I0577425

David Lean
and his films

Alain Silver and James Ursini

David Lean

and his films

Leslie Frewin of London

© Alain Silver and James Ursini, 1974

First published in 1974 by
Leslie Frewin Publishers Limited,
Five Goodwin's Court, Saint Martin's Lane,
London WC2N 4LL, England.

Designed by Craig Dodd

Photoset, printed and bound in England
by Weatherby Woolnough, Sanders Road,
Wellingborough, Northamptonshire.

ISBN 0 85632 095 1

. . . David Lean is a poet
and imagist . . .
Robert Bolt

David Lean and his films
have won twenty-five 'Oscars' awarded by
The American Academy of Motion Picture Arts and Sciences
and ten awards of
The British Society of Film and Television Arts.
He was the recipient of a Life Fellowship
of SFTA in 1974.

Contents

List of Illustrations

Introduction

IT IS NO easy task to place David Lean in any directorial hierarchy, to give him a number in some arbitary rating system; nor is it necessarily advisable to do so. Historically, Lean's stature as a director is almost unparalleled. There is no other whose very name can command more money or resources than his. More importantly, no other director of any rank can claim to put more physical time and energy into a project – practically a literal twenty-four hours a day – can be more in dread of the personal 'death' that occurs at the completion of each film or more plagued by a compulsive perfectionism* that prolongs production in futile hope of avoiding that inevitable end. And yet Lean would probably never call himself more than competent, an artisan perhaps, but primarily a good inventor of photographic images who gets things done.

Our aim is not, however, to psychoanalyze Lean. The major interest here (and ultimately that which may reveal most about the man as well) is his work. For those fifteen motion pictures, more than anything else, contradict any allegations that David Lean is less than an artist.

* Claude Chabrol has remarked that he and David Lean are the only directors who will wait forever for a perfect sunset – 'forever,' for Chabrol, being in the context of a six-week shooting schedule; for Lean, a part of six years' work.

Andre Bazin has divided film reality into three conceivable forms: "(1) *A purely logical and descriptive analysis* . . . (2) *A psychological analysis,* from within the film, namely one that fits the point of view of one of the protagonists in a given situation . . . (3) *A psychological analysis from the point of view of the spectator.*"* To de-limit these types slightly, one might class them simply as objective, subjective, or ironic respectively. As a director Lean may (must) deal with all these "realities," often within a given film, must (as they are the only possible modes) define his "vision" through them.

Oliver Twist (1948) is a prime illustration. In the shots of the workhouse, Lean delineates a basic 'reality.' His direction here is objective (although there are ironies in the very design of the set and the superimposed title) aimed at establishing the narrative core of the film. But in setting distance or angle, he may add to the material reality of image, something of the emotional (character) reality not 'physically' present. As in the high angle medium shot of the boys drawing straws: when they leave, amidst hushed cries, Oliver is alone – his sensation is visualized by the isolation of his white-gowned figure within the gray confines of the frame and the two-dimensional reduction in height, the 'flattening' imposed by placing the camera above him. Or by focusing on an image within the general expository necessity of the scene, Lean may underscore its dramatic (serious or comic) quality. The only necessary images in the sequence of Nancy's murder, for example, are those which make it clear that Sikes has killed her. Beyond that Lean may single out, still within the context of observable detail,† a specific image such as the close shot of Sikes' dog scratching furiously at the door. The obvious analytical point – that the episode is terrifying because the dog wants desperately to get out – is made by a selective rather than substantive

* *What is Cinema?* translated by Hugh Gray, University of California Press (1967).

† The point to make clear here is that the fiction assumes a basic suspension of disbelief. Hence, the spectator sitting down to view the film will not be unduly surprised to discover a world of only black and white with characters dressed in and housed in early Victorian fashion, in short a world entirely incongruous with the one outside the theater. Murder and the fixtures of a room are potentially equal as observable realities, if different on a dramatic level, just as they are beyond the confines of the movie house.

10

manipulation within the fixed reality of the scene. In spying through a glass port on Monks and Fagin in the back of a tavern, Nancy takes in everything she can but her view of the complete 'picture' is restricted. Analogously, the 'objective plane' – that which provides the basic information – in a film is not aligned to any pre-determined standards (neither induced from the general objectivity of the whole of cinema nor reasoned out *a priori*) but derived from the specific 'vantage' set up by the director. And the definition of that objective plane, for want of a better term, the *mise-en-scene*, may be taken as the first component of directional style.

That style is further refined in a substantive manner, by what Bazin calls 'fit[ting on] the point of view of one of the protagonists.' Instances of direct 'point of view' from *Oliver Twist* are strikingly recorded when the camera 'becomes' Oliver fleeing a crowd of pursuers: travelling forward rapidly, it slips, at his eye level, through the arms of one man then runs into the clenched fist of another, whereupon it 'loses consciousness' by means of a cut to black. Later, in the court-room, it will sway dizzily (an effect accentuated by using a wide-angle rather than a normal lens), blur in and out of focus, and finally fall over in a faint. Here an objective view of the world is physically displaced.

Going back for a moment, consider again the shot of Oliver alone after drawing the short straw. Was it truly objective, or did the staging take it beyond a simple witnessing of a narrative event? A clearer answer may be found in the opening sequence of the film. On a country road in the midst of a sudden storm, Oliver's mother begins to give birth to him. In one travelling in, Lean simultaneously records the labor objectively (a medium shot to medium close shot, her body arched, head tilted back, grimacing) and totally externalizes not just the intangible emotion of her plight but the physical sensation too. Knifing pain is equated to a white sheet of lightning; a contorting spasm is captured by an angular tilt from horizontal which levels off as the contraction subsides; her complete disorientation and the distortion of her real perceptions are characterized by making her walk on a treadmill before a process screen, which device

11

makes her move unnaturally at the edge of consciousness and introduces a secondary 'reality' of reduced dimension behind the already existing one of the film itself.

Beyond this intricate subjectification, Lean may compound the frame's reality with dramatic irony. This is classically accomplished in the sequence where Nancy is followed by the Artful Dodger – the audience being privileged to observe through several shots of him lurking outside the house and trailing behind her down the rainy streets, something of vital concern that she is unaware of. Lean can also fashion a subtler ironic mode on a figurative level: as in the first conversation between Monks and Fagin in the garret. Here while Fagin's eyes stay on his body moving in and out of shot, Monks becomes momentarily for the audience a thin, black shadow on the right side of the frame. This stylized rendering of Monk's form implies his malevolent character as well as the manner in which his presence looms ominously over the entire picture, a 'fact' which Fagin (as the shadow is not in his line of sight) cannot know.

*   *   *   *   *

All this should briefly have suggested something of the awareness of the medium which Lean brings to his material. Yet, of late, David Lean has become a target of critical disfavor. He is accused of 'cold-hearted' technique, of lack of personality, and of shallow and unsubtle ideas. Though they cannot deny that his films are immaculately finished works, critics frequently assess them as slick appeals to emotionalism harbored in pictorial quaintness. However, their real problem with Lean is simple: how to cope with his unfailing popularity. For the phenomenal amounts his pictures earn at the box-office and the praise of his peers in the industry (evidenced in the scores of international citations and the astonishing number of British and American awards he has received) may provoke a kind of petty jealousy, a lingering resentment of success seeking justification in the rationalization that 'he can't be *that* good,' that someone who is this much of a craftsman and entertainer cannot possibly possess the depth of a Bergman or an Antonioni.

12

It is difficult to imagine even a superficial analysis of this man's films that does not reveal an intensely personal and dedicated director. After breaking the theatrical yoke imposed by Noel Coward in his first three films, Lean's motion pictures began consistently to express a multi-faceted and complex view of life and art. It is not the purpose of this study to polemicize or formulate responses to those who do not perceive this. Nor is it to venture too broadly into the shadowy remains of critical theory and argue questions of aesthetic depth or self-conscious artistry. It may contend that Lean draws, consciously or unconsciously, on Romantic or Pantheistic notions for his thematic inspiration, that his films (all of which he writes or rewrites to a substantial degree though most often uncredited) are verbally and visually fashioned from particular individual as well as archetypal concepts. It may, at times, take I. A. Richards' suggestion and attempt, in picking out those archetypes or non-referential images, to analyze Lean's method of communicating sensation as well as narrative line. But it will not rigidly adhere to any formal pre-conceptions. *Auteurism* would tie us to tracing an imposition of a homogeneous 'style' over all his projects, in the face of equally lucid arguments that form must bend to content or that both are inextricably bound up in a complicated symbiosis of reflexive definition and other complementary factors. At the same time, a detached and independent examination of each film (under the pretense, say, of each having been fashioned by many anonymous hands) would not only make it unreasonable to speak of clear and sometimes pre-eminent thematic amplifications and developments but also would eliminate the possibility of exploring the thrust of recurring images as Lean's personal patterns of expression refined over the whole of his creative output.

We do not put forth these disavowals of existing theories as groundwork for any counter-assertion of 'Objectivity.' This is not an objective book. Considering a man's life, it might with effort remain a purely factual account. Directed as it is almost exclusively at his work, it cannot be so. Its interpretations, general and specific, are based on subjective tastes and perceptions. Hopefully, that will not prevent them from being,

13

occasionally at least, relevant or revealing. Moreover, between assessment of a given film in terms of good and bad or simply clarifying how it functions as something with a language and grammar of its own, the emphasis is heavily on the latter.

Accordingly, this introduction has been written not merely to define our basic approaches, but to confront all the contrarious abstractions and to move beyond. Its intent was not to supersede existing critical currencies but to set their valuations and their rates of exchange aside for a moment, in order to get down to the 'goods' themselves.

Chapter 1

The Early Films:
IN WHICH WE SERVE (1942);
THIS HAPPY BREED (1944);
BLITHE SPIRIT (1945)

The sun was shining on the sea,
Shining with all his might:
He did his very best to make
The billows smooth and bright.

*Lewis Carroll, 'The Walrus
and the Carpenter'*

No coward soul is mine,
No trembler in the world's storm-
troubled sphere.

Emily Bronte

IN WHICH WE SERVE is only one in a long list of propaganda films turned out by England and the United States during World War II. Based on the actual service record of a British destroyer (recounted to Noel Coward by Lord Mountbatten), it advances the standard line of support for the war effort and follows a familiar pattern by combining the story of H.M.S. Torrin, from shipyard to the bottom of the Mediterranean Sea, with the personal lives of its captain and crew. Yet, within this context, the film

15

has its reputation. And if it seems, at times, cloying or overeager on its way to the message of the closing title ('God bless our ships and all who sail on them.'), it remains significant not just as David Lean's first try at directing, but as a picture singled out for admiration by its contempories amid scores of similar efforts.

Upon entering the film industry at the age of nineteen, in 1927, Lean was employed at various positions from messenger boy through assistant director to editor. With the advent of sound Lean's knowledge of synchronization secured him succeeding positions as chief editor for a number of studios. [See Appendix]. By the end of the 1930's, he was the most respected and highest paid editor in Britain. His work (in such films as *Pygmalion, Major Barbara,* and *49th Parallel*) was singled out for the classical economy of the cutting and the dynamism of the dramatic montages. With these excellent references, Coward found Lean a natural choice to aid him with the technical aspects of *In Which We Serve.* After a few weeks of shooting, Coward lost interest in what he called the 'fussiness' of film direction and turned the reins over to Lean. Except for suggestions regarding performances, Lean was left in charge. But, in all, he was still little more than a technician with the assigned task of faithfully translating Coward's ideas and characterizations into more or less cinematic terms.

The opening sequence ('This is the story of a ship') is a succinct, almost documentary montage. In the shipyard, cuts of girders dropping into place, hot rivets being passed, and sweating workmen are juxtaposed to create a condensed but kaleidoscopic view of the construction. As the ship is completed dissolves reveal the Torrin slipping out of drydock for her sea-trial accompanied by an exultant surge of music and the Union Jack being raised in the near foreground of a high angle long shot.

During the ship's return home, after a near-fatal skirmish, Lean similarly eliminates long, dull stretches of exposition by isolating bits and pieces of the journey. Much of this emphasis on a visual development of the action is reminiscent of *One Of Our Aircraft Is Missing,* a picture edited by Lean a year earlier. In the battle scenes, reaction shots intercut

16

with anti-aircraft guns bursting, shouts mixed with shells exploding on the track, energetically define the chaos. In the subsequent reflective calm as the Torrin limps back to port, static medium and medium close shots avoid any false anti-climaxes and allow for a dramatic detente.

Most of the film is constructed from various flashbacks as the Torrin's sailors float in and around a tiny life-raft within sight of the ravaged and slowly sinking ship. From this core Lean elaborates both the individual stories and the Torrin's history along parallel lines. From the men's weary, oil-stained faces, he dissolves back to both domestic scenes and earlier events aboard the vessel. But these interwoven flashbacks are also one of *In Which We Serve*'s major inconsistencies. Their purpose is ostensibly to allow each character remembering the events to tell his own story, from his point of view. A number of perspectives of one incident may be given; but although the flashback begins in the context of one person's memories, it often ends in the middle of another's. Events that the character who is 'remembering' was not involved in are somehow conjured up (for example, all three Christmas dinners are in Captain Kinross' flashback, although he was present at only one of them). Or, as the personal stories are somewhat interrelated, occurences leading up to climactic moments (e.g. Blake telling Hardy of his wife's death) may be divided between two flash-backs irregardless of who was actually privy to them. In short, the 'subjectivity' (a quality on which Lean will come to place particular stress) of the various remembrances is repeatedly violated.

Beyond this tangle of memories, another weak contrivance is that inter-working of individual histories. The manner of Blake's chance meeting with Freda on the train and the fact that she is related to his petty officer by marriage are initial coincidences, which are augmented by Shorty's remark that his parents met in a similar fashion. Further, on their trip to Torquay after their wedding, the Blakes just happen to encounter Kinross and his wife, who in their turn muse over their own honeymoon voyage taken years before to the same destination. Much of Coward's literary irony and calculated understatement derives from this kind of plot manipulation. But Lean manages to add the same qualities on a visual level while partially circumventing the web of narrative complications. From a slow travelling in towards a newspaper announcing, 'No War This Year,' Lean cuts to a sea battle off Crete, with the detached, matter-of-fact flavor of the explanatory title: 'Crete. May 23, 1941.' accenting the lack of emotionalism. There is the same 'anti-momentous' impact, over space rather than time, in a cut from Mrs. Kinross reading her children lines from 'The Walrus and the Carpenter' to a depth charge disturbing the 'billows, smooth and bright.' In both instances, Lean creates an ironic synthesis from the opposition of single images. On a more complex level, there is the Kinross family picnic: isolated on a rural hillside, the outing is interrupted by the appearance of several fighter planes. The scene follows one of Chief Hardy and his family viewing a newsreel of the war; the structure here is much like that of a sequence in *Brief Encounter,* moving from a theatre (representing artificiality) to the outdoors (naturalness). But the natural elements of open field and sky are abruptly superseded by the inescapable, mechanistic devices of war. The personal idyll (the first of many in Lean's work) is disrupted, as the family is made to witness a dogfight, a combat of moth-like, faceless gladiators in the no longer peaceful heavens.

In Which We Serve also gives first evidence of an awareness of camera movement and composition. When Shorty and Freda rest in a tea room, Lean distills the essense of sentimental, middle-class courtship into a single medium close two-shot, partially silhouetted against a window (anticipating like scenes in both *Brief Encounter* and *Great Expectations*). As the crew participates in a dedication service, he uses a slow travelling to scan and unite the entire company, moving across the assembly into a medium close shot of Kinross (the visual and moral center) then back again in a reflexive action. The long take as Mrs. Kinross expresses her begrudging admiration for her husband's ship or the tracking into Kinross as he delivers his farewell address are equally direct stagings which appropriately underscore without overemphasizing the dramatic tensions of their respective scenes.

18

n Which We Serve

Richard Attenborough in *In Which We Serve*

Above: Celia Johnson.

Below: Noel Coward, Celia Johnson and the rest of the Kinross family.

Above: Noel Coward and John Mills.

Below: Noel Coward, as Captain Kinross.

John Mills as Shorty.

Lean may indulge in visual flourishes, such as the tracking shot into the tattoo ('Freda') on Shorty's forearm or the Blake wedding party posing for a photograph and reflected in the lens of the still camera, but not very frequently. And it may be, as with the rippling effect superimposed over several transitions, to a definite purpose—in this case, a simulation of the sensation of drowning (to the point of having the rippling 'uncontrollably' appear and fade in the middle of flashback dialogue) and the justification for the flashback itself (a man's life passing before his eyes). But the most dynamic sequence in the film, the death of Mrs. Hardy and her mother and the subsequent birth of Freda's baby, is a simple, uncluttered assemblage of shots. From the bombers flying over the Hardy house, the scene moves directly to a medium close shot of Mrs. Hardy and her mother huddled in the foreground with Freda nearby under a stairwell. Suddenly within the same shot, a bomb explodes and the building is destroyed. Only Freda is saved. Immediately after, she gives birth, an event which Lean amplifies with a panorama of the ocean and seabirds in flight. It becomes the earliest example of a birth-death cycle which Lean will set in motion again and again in later pictures.

*　　*　　*　　*　　*

As a result of this film, Lean, Ronald Neame (the cinematographer), and Anthony Havelock-Allan (the associate producer) formed, with Coward's assistance, an independent production company called Cineguild (which was to produce all of Lean's motion pictures up to and including *Madeleine*).

With the success, both critical and financial, of *In Which We Serve,* Cineguild was on solid ground. The immediate program was not a highly speculative one: three more Coward films, taken from his stage plays. Although Lean, Neame, and Havelock-Allan would share adaptation credit on all of them and perform the various production chores behind the back of the playwright (who was also producer) so to speak, the emphasis remained firmly on Coward. With his name coming at the end of the main titles (contrary to the traditional placing of the director's name last) and even remaining on the screen for a bit longer (on *Blithe Spirit*, for instance, Lean as director and Neame as cinematographer both have their own cards which run for seven feet; Coward's follows for nine), it was clearly 'Noel Coward's *Blithe Spirit*, or *This Happy Breed* and not 'David Lean's film of.' Nor could it really have been otherwise for the fledgling members of Cineguild. For Rank, within its enlightened policy of handing money over to such satellite production units as Cineguild, Two Cities (Coward's company), or the Archers (Michael Powell and Emeric Pressburger), would be rather more willing to continue its backing if they stuck to what they knew. And what they knew, for the moment at least, was Noel Coward.

The film to follow in the wake of H.M.S. Torrin was *This Happy Breed.* Begun just months after the stage production, it derives from an original that might be called a semi-sequel to Coward's classic *Cavalcade.* It spans the subsequent two decades from 1919 to 1939, while concentrating again on the personal history of an English family. However, *This Happy Breed's* middle-class, ostensibly 'democratic' members do not really follow in the bourgeois Victorian, support-the-empire traditions of Coward's previous success. Beyond that *This Happy Breed,* which ended on a roughly contemporary date, focused on a past too immediate and too full of the bitter memories of depression and Red Scare, too flavored by the hindsight ironies of appeasement to give rise to nostalgic reminiscence. Much more distinguished the reign of Edward from that of Victoria than an added half-century on a throne; there was also the difference between tea in the dining room and chaw in the parlor, between the florid manners of Victorian gentility and the boisterousness of the working class at home.

This Happy Breed does bear some genuine resemblance to *In Which We Serve,* specifically to the domestic scenes of the Hardys and the Blakes. The inhabitants of Number Seventeen Sycamore Road, Clapham Common are much the same people, with their irritable in-laws, their just-plain-folks camaraderie, and their unshakeable belief that no matter how hard the times Mother England is forged of good stock and somehow common sense will prevail. 'The people themselves, the ordinary people like you and me,' Frank Gibbons tells his infant grandson, 'we know what what we belong to, where we come from, and where we're going. We may not know it with our brains, but we know it with our roots.'

The entire play is fashioned from a simple conceit: within the context of naturalistic dialogue and decor, it proceeds to pick out the nine key scenes, the climactic or transcendent moments of a half-dozen lives over a span of twenty years. The classic problem in transposing material of this variety to the screen is how to treat the episodic structure – whether to fill it in with other scenes and transitional montages or leave it precisely as written enforcing the sensation of photographed stage play. In addition, a host of secondary considerations, such as dialogue style, must be dealt with. For while Coward makes sure that all the correct 'h's' are dropped, the demands of the narrative necessitate a good many blatantly expository remarks and exchanges not made for the benefit of the character(s) to whom they are addressed but designed primarily to inform the audience of certain events. That, in turn, brings up the intricate questions of stage audience versus film audience, proscenium arch versus Academy ratio, theater lights versus Technicolor.

Bazin, deeply mired in these concerns, wrote in his essay on 'Theater and Cinema' that 'however one approaches it, a play whether classic or modern is unassailably protected by its text. There is no way of adapting the text without disposing of it and substituting something else, which may be better, but is not the play.' Clearly, the aim of the adaptors of both *This Happy Breed* and *Blithe Spirit* was not to supersede the text. The essential issue then becomes not how to deal with actual lines and scenes, but with basic qualities, with what the play has that the film can render better. The results, in *This Happy Breed,* are not wholly satisfactory. For the film itself emerges as episodic without effect, calculatedly detailed under a semblance of accidental observation, a narrative of fits and starts as characters try to become people and people never succeed in becoming characters.

The primary reason for this, aside from the aforementioned conven-

25

tional problems, is the handicap of realism. What the adaptors try to give the motion picture *This Happy Breed* and what unltimately causes it to fail is more 'credibility,' more documentary reality than it can support. Under the camera eye, in Three-strip Technicolor,* the Gibbons family ceases to be an assemblage of stage figures seen at a distance and becomes graphically real. The aging that takes place between acts is a simple illusion on stage. On film, in close-up, the faces of Frank and Ethel have the authenticity of well-defined wrinkles framed by hair with subtler streaks of grey. The gradual stoop of Celia Johnson's (Ethel's) shoulders under the weight of passing years is as noticeable as the changing style of her dresses (which always retain the dowdiness befitting her station). Yet all this and a few shots of the 'row' houses on Sycamore Road, giving the fictional Number 17 a physical presence it could never have on stage, still do not make those who dwell there substantively real.

Much of the difficulty does lie with the original, with its sterile half-truths and rigid slice-of-life posings. Many of its supporting characters are hopelessly one-dimensional, thin as well as flat. Here the film improves, particularly in the case of Bob Mitchell, making the 'chum from the war' less of a drinking partner and general foil and more of an alternate resident of Sycamore Road. The film can also add some wry touches either by shifting a scene (for example, Frank's pre-marital lecture to Reg in the parlor, now takes place in the lavatory, which makes their figures seem somewhat incongruous in their formal clothes and comically underscores the pompous aspect of his advice) or by inventing a new one (the trip to the cinema to see the incomprehensible American picture suggesting the intolerant remnants of Victorian xenophobia). It can even make a small detail, such as Ethel taking down Edward's calendar after the abdication, which may have seemed too contrived in the play, a more spontaneous and acceptable action.

---

* Although the added expense of using this process may seem unusual, it was consistent with industry policy of generally restricting color to 'theatrical' material, where studio photography would predominate and the potentially costly and uncontrollable factors involved in exterior work could be avoided. In 'opening up' the play, however, Cineguild did add several exterior sequences.

The major action, however, must continue to center on characters who do not speak words but utter lines of dialogue. Bazin's dictum holds true: the text cannot be merely appended with film effects or partially displaced by movie reality. The opening shots of the city and the travelling into the house establish one reality; then the 'play' begins and asserts another. A view of the mob of people greeting Chamberlain at 10 Downing Street compounds the irony of Frank's remark ('It's exciting all right, if you like to see a lot of people yelling themselves hoarse without the faintest idea what they're yelling about.') but subverts its drama. For Coward's personnages are not just any inhabitants of Clapham Common, they are *the* inhabitants of Clapham Common. They are nothing more or less than lumps of observed traits, everymen and women mouthing uncertain epithets of earthly wisdom and, as such, not meant to venture out of the dramatic insulation of three walls of a parlor. They are, like Frank Gibbons framed in medium shot between his sister and daughter rolling up yarn, trapped by a graphically mundane reality that is not inherently theirs.

Blithe Spirit is, if nothing else, a radical departure from the mundane. Coward subtitled his play 'An Improbable Farce in Three Acts,' but it might more accurately be termed a drawing room comedy (literally so in its original theatrical conception which restricts it to that one room) of the supernatural. As a comedy, it stands almost alone in Lean's work (his only other effort in a generally comic vein being *Hobson's Choice*); but its a typicality, the scarcity of elements that are distinctively Lean's, only starts there.

It is clear from the beginning that *Blithe Spirit* is basically Coward's picture. His written preface:

> When we are young
> We read and believe
> The most fantastic things
> When we grow older and wiser
> We learn with perhaps a little regret
> That these things can never be.

This Happy Breed

Celia Johnson as Ethel Gibbons in *This Happy Breed*

Above: Celia Johnson with Robert Newton as husband and wife, Ethel and Frank Gibbons.

Below: Celia Johnson and John Mills.

is qualified by his own voice on the track saying, 'We are quite, quite wrong.' The characters who will prove this – bored ('Not by the wildest stretch of the imagination could you describe it as the first fine careless rapture,'), politely insulting ('You have a genius for understatement.') snobs ('That remark comes perilously close to impertinence.') – flaunt the archetypal traits of the English petty aristocracy. And since, as usual, Coward draws his effects from their wry exaggeration, it becomes essential to the comedy of the film as much as it was to that of the play that the twice-widowered Charles Condomine and his wives Elvira and Ruth (dead in that order) remain faithful to his conception.

Accordingly, the movie Charles Condomine is still the sophisticated foil of Coward's invention, adept at the well-turned, Wildesian phrase (Charles: 'It's discouraging to think how many people are shocked by honesty and how few by deceit.') and the sublimely egotistic comebacker (Ruth: 'Write that down, you might forget it.' Charles: 'You underrate me.'). When Madame Arcati, the haphazard medium, complains of a premonition that has not panned out ('I thought I was going to have a puncture so I went back to fetch my pump – and then, of course, I didn't.'), Charles is ever ready with the gracious good word ('Perhaps you will on the way home.'). But at heart he is true to a tradition of insensitive materialism (as his 'Hmm, we must keep Edith in the house more' when he hears of a former servant girl's indiscretion or his exploitation of Arcati to research a book demonstrate). The idiosyncrasy he shares with the likes of Frank Gibbons is that firm belief that the logical order of things is not easily subverted ('Why should having a cheese thing for lunch make me see my deceased wife after dinner?'), which can lead to only one conclusion when it finally and irrefutably is: 'I've gone mad – that's what it is. I've just gone raving mad.' In Coward's scheme, Charles is more prone to make the amusing 'remark of a pompous ass' than an uproarious joke. Against what Elvira terms his 'certain seedy grandeur' are arrayed the almost standard devices, such as the ongoing malentendu of saying unpleasant things to a ghost and having another character present think it directed at them. Further antagonism is provided by Madame Arcati. Strengthened by her giddy naturalness and sensory awareness ('It was wonderful cycling through the woods, I was deafened by birdsong.'), she contrasts with Charles' mannered artificiality ('Experience has taught me to be wary of concoctions.') and attacks his triteness by a process of reversal ('Well, Madame Arcati, the time is drawing near.' 'Who knows . . . it may be receding.'). The cumulative result, on a narrative level, is a play that is funny without being very imaginative. But the film manages, here and there, to inject a bit of the latter quality without compromising the former.

Bazin proposes that the first thought of many directors in adapting a piece is to 'conceal the theater,' to 'overcompensate by the "superiority" of its [the cinema's] technique – which in turn is mistaken for aesthetic superiority,'* in short, to open it up. Lean does not over compensate. There are some added bits (the comic dissolve from Arcati's 'Oh, no red meat, I hope. I make it a rule never to eat red meat before I work,' to a close shot of a bloody slice of roast beef being carved and passed to her; the invisible Elvira driving Charles' roadster to the bewilderment of a traffic controller; or a shot of Arcati's parrot chirping, 'Poltergeist, pretty Poltergeist.'), but they are few and peripheral. Even the special effects are fairly restrained. The floating objects and doors opening by themselves are really nothing more than wired stagecraft. And the transparent Elvira in her glowing green gown, entering suddenly via the closed French windows or having her hair disarranged as Ruth runs through her on the stairs, is a simple movie illusion.

Lean is equally restrained in his choice of angles. The sets have a

* The reason for this, Bazin postulates, is that, 'the preconceptions of the public in these matters serve to confirm those of the filmmakers. People in general do not give much thought to the cinema. For them it means vast decor, plenty of action, and exteriors. If they are not given a minimum of what they call cinema, they feel cheated. The cinema must be more lavish than the theater.' Alfred Hitchcock summarizes the formula for injecting 'lavishness' in this way: 'Here's the usual method: in the play a character arrives from outside and he comes by taxi; so, in the film, the adaptors show you the taxi's arrival, the characters getting out, walking up, climbing stairs, knocking at a door, and entering the room. At that point a long scene from the play begins, and if the character talks about a trip, they seize the occasion to show it to us through flashback. They forget, in this way, that the fundamental quality of the play is in its concentration.'

31

theatrical depth, but the camera placement does not exploit it. Rather, the interplay between foreground and background is severely curtailed and reserved for certain useful touches: the two ghostly wives waiting impatiently on a settee while the ineffectual Arcati clambers up a ladder in the center of the room; or a medium close two shot of Ruth looking from Charles to an empty space in the background where Elvira would be if she could be seen. In the medium and long shots, characters are generally fixed in the same plane in relation to the camera (i.e. in two shots the stage line is usually at 90° to the camera's line of sight instead of favoring one figure over the other's shoulder), a direct and uncluttered staging, which flattens perspective and restricts interest to the frame's foreground. Further, most medium close-ups are straight on and used for reactions, the banter being delivered in medium and group shots (the cocktail sequence with the Bradmans, for example, is made up of thirteen cuts with medium and medium long angles prevailing in eleven of them). Even when it tracks from a two shot of Elvira stroking Charles' head, through the hall doors (which part for it to pass), pausing to glance at a mirror which reflects both figures in the parlor (also implying that somehow Elvira *is* physically present), and up to a clock, the camera continues to function as an objective and somewhat ironic 'third person.'

Throughout Lean eschews any flourishes in approaching the material. He may tamper with the time sense of the original, but only for a purpose. As Charles and Ruth argue over the 'reality' of Elvira, he employs a series of dissolves over time (from morning to evening) and place (from dining room to hall to supper table to coffee on the terrace) and, in so doing, infuses their purely theatrical exasperation with a growing intensity. His two inserts of a clock at 4:15 and 4:30 in the final exorcism scenes emphasize the subjectivity of the various characters' sensation of 'endlessness.'

Most of Lean's interpretations of the text are of this sort. He underscores selected elements of genre satire (Arcati's mock-spectral shadow magnified on the wall in her pre-trance flitting about; the build-up of paraphernalia in the exorcism including a close shot of an urn that

lithe Spirit

 shadow of Madame Arcarti (Maragaret Rutherford) rivets the attention of Rex Harrison, Constance
 nmings, Hugh Wakefield and Joyce Carey in *Blithe Spirit*

Above: Margaret Rutherford, Hugh Wakefield, Constance Cummings, Rex Harrison and Joyce Carey.

Below: Kay Hammond and Constance Cummings.

Above: Constance Cummings, Kay Hammond and Rex Harrison.

Below: Kay Hammond—the 'ghost' of the title – with Rex Harrison.

'smokes' mothballs) but only lightly. His actual 'special effects' are derived from the editing. On a direct level, Lean adds visual humor in a cut from Arcati's 'It upsets my vibrations' to a tea-kettle boiling and whistling. The tightening from medium to close two shot and holding for ten lines as Charles quizzes Elvira on what she has done to the car is an early instance of Lean's translating dramatic apprehension into a sensible, visual correlative, narrowing the angle and withholding the cut until the emotional anxiety is dissipated (with Elvira's succession of hapless 'oh's'). Lean makes fullest use of 'technique' when Elvira demonstrates to Ruth that she is far from imaginary. The progression of details (flowers in mid-air; Elvira menacingly raising a chair over her head; curtains pulled shut; an ornament hurled from the mantel; a door thrown open), all flawlessly timed, are gradually intercut with close shots of the two women. The notion of confrontation is sharpened and concentrated, until Ruth runs out screaming in capitulation and a cut to long shot again co-incides with a release of tension.

*   *   *   *   *

The question of style is never a simple one, except perhaps in its absense, if that is possible. Yet there is something of Lean present in *This Happy Breed* and *Blithe Spirit.* Perhaps, again, it is little more than an application of craft. Thematically, beyond limited aspects of Madame Arcati and her breathless inquiries about 'No sudden gusts of cold wind, I hope?' or Queenie in *This Happy Breed* with her 'highfalutin' ideas' ('I want too much – I'm always thinking about the things I want.'), there is little that anticipates later work. And the one major alteration in *Blithe Spirit* – a new ending in which Charles goes to meet his wives in the 'echoing vaults of eternity' – seems less to have been the personal inspiration of any of the adaptors than a matter of rounding out the retribution for questionable motives and morals.

But this shouldn't imply that all the merit or lack of it in these two pictures was Coward's responsibility, or that credit or blame should not be divided with the other members of Cineguild. And certainly a good

36

deal of *Blithe Spirit*'s success was determined not just by the production unit, nor by Rex Harrison's much-praised incarnation of Charles Condomine, but also by Kay Hammond's throaty Elvira and Margaret Rutherford's dotty Arcati (both practiced performances from the stage version).

After three pictures, Lean had no particular desire to continue shining on *Coward's* sea, to go on doing *his* best to make another's billows smooth and bright.* Nor was he alone in this – Neame and Havelock-Allan were also tired of being junior partners. But before parting company, they had one more Coward project to film.

* According to Neame: 'David had always wanted to do something other than a stage play. We decided we had to prove ourselves apart from Coward [because] any Noel Coward film must be primarily a Noel Coward film, and we wanted to try our own wings.'

Chapter 2

BRIEF ENCOUNTER (1945)

When I behold, upon the night's starr'd face,
Huge cloudy symbols of high romance,
And feel that I may never live to trace
Their shadows, with the magic hand of chance;
And when I feel, fair creature of an hour;
That I shall never look upon thee more,
Never have relish in the faery power
Of unreflecting love! – then on the shore
Of the wide world I stand alone, and think
Till Love and Fame to nothingness do sink.

*John Keats, 'When I
have fears that I may
cease to be'*

BRIEF ENCOUNTER IS not only Lean's first major success both in popular and critical terms but is, in form and content, seminal to the rest of his creative output. While many of Coward's ideas might not appear to be basically in line with Lean's – he never returned to the ironic drawing room comedy (*Blithe Spirit*), the patriotic war film (*In Which We Serve*), or the expansive history of an English family (*This Happy Breed*) – this particular story, a short-lived quasi-adulterous romance between two ostensibly ordinary people, will reappear in varying forms throughout Lean's work.

The source of *Brief Encounter* was Noel Coward's play *Still Life.* The first step of the screen adaptors (Lean, Neame, Havelock Allan, and Coward himself) was towards opening the play up. In keeping with Lean's considerable drive to enlarge outwardly and escape the studio (that 'dark hole' as he calls it), the film now spread beyond the railroad station tea room, which contained almost all the action of the original, to the city streets, a train platform, woods, park gardens, and a picturesque countryside. Moreover, this exterior expansion lended itself to the development of pantheistic imagery which Lean would begin, with this film, to consistently apply to his projects.

In Lean's motion pictures the forces of nature are meaningful participants in the lives of the characters. Every inner emotion or outward action is echoed, complemented, even spurred on by natural phenomena. As Wordsworth's nature was infused with a 'sense sublime,' so is Lean's. As Wordsworth placed man in the continuum of Self and Nature ('To her fair works did Nature link/The human soul that through me ran,' [*Lines written in Early Spring*]) so does Lean. In the Romantic tradition which Lean assimilates, everything is, transcendentally, a part of the same Spirit. It is, in this light, only reasonable to assume that each part should interreact with and color the other.

To escape their 'ordinary' lives and find the kind of 'High romance' Keats speaks of, Alec Harvey and Laura Jesson return to nature. They go first to the Botanical Gardens, then to the river, and finally to a quaint bridge near a wooded area to (as Wordsworth again might put it) 'Come forth into the light of things, and let Nature be your teacher' (*The Tables Turned*). Here their love ripens in idyllic communion with their surroundings. They even rent a boat and let the flow of the river determine their course – only to be halted when a man-made barrier (a bridge over a dam) bars their progress. On a symbolic level, this obs-

40

truction represents all the repressive conventions society has arrayed against them – the artificial sense of propriety, the duty to class and family, and the resultant sexual guilt – everything that stops up the course of the river, that prevents nature from teaching them. The effect these 'damming' inhibitions (Alec: 'The feeling of guilt in doing wrong is too strong, isn't it? Too great a price to pay for the happiness we have together.') have on Laura is epitomized in the scene following the lovers' third meeting. On the train she squirms in her seat trying to avoid the eyes of a minister in her compartment whom she imagines is somehow aware of her 'sin.' She returns home to find her child hurt in an accident. In voice-over, she remembers (hovering over his bed, terrified): 'I tried not to show it, but I was quite hysterical inside . . . as though the whole thing were my fault . . . a sort of punishment, an awful, sinister warning.' It is 'unnatural' apprehensions of this sort which will end the affair.

The wind has always taken on a metaphysical implications in Romantic and Symbolist poetry. From Coleridge's 'Eolian Harp' through Shelley's 'Ode to the West Wind' to Yeats' 'To a Child Dancing in the Wind,' it may be viewed alternately as a source of inspiration and as an omen of doom. Lean's use of it is particularly representative of this dual concept of a both beneficient and malevolent force.* Alec and Laura's first kiss occurs in a darkly-lit alley and is played against the rush of wind generated by a passing train. Though the train itself is an example of fairly obvious sexual symbolism, the wind (in this scene; in the later cloudburst during the lovers' emotionally stormy rendezvous at the flat; at Laura's near suicide) acts to heighten the Romantic mood and elevate the commonplace occurrence. At the same time, it adds preter-natural dimension to the scene – as if the whole animated cosmos, even the man-made moving parts of it (trains, and the like), participated in their love affair, in their 'overwhelming feeling' (Alec's words). Admittedly, the nature symbolism is not as dominant in this film as it will be in future

---

* A notion most effectively described by Mary Shelley: 'Then mighty are thou, O wind, to be throned above all other vicegerents of nature's power; whether thou comes destroying from the east, or pregnant with elementary life from the west; thee the clouds obey; the sun is subservient to thee; the shoreless ocean is thy slave.' (*The Last Man*)

others. But it is a key concept – central to both the narrative development and selection of figurative images – and attests to Lean's ability to infuse a scene with his 'flowering' pantheism.

*   *   *   *   *

The technique of subjectification which was used, perhaps somewhat unclearly, in *In Which We Serve* has been largely perfected by *Brief Encounter.* The opening and closing sequences in the tea shop demonstrate very effectively the use Lean and Coward make of this device. The scene opens as two of the film's comic relief characters, the station attendant and the bar hostess, indulge in some humorous sexual banter, their mock courtship ironically sounding the main theme. As the camera noncommittedly records these happenings, a shop girl enters the frame. The camera follows her around the bar and in the background there are two people (Alec and Laura), sitting at a corner table sadly silent, occasionally gazing into each other's eyes. The girl leaves the frame and the camera holds on them in medium shot, but only momentarily, then cuts back to the attendant and hostess. The shots in this scene are composed so that Alec and Laura take on no more importance than any other background character or object in the tea room. As the hostess delivers her last quip, directed at the station attendant ('Time and tide wait for no man' – acting also as a wry comment on the situation at that corner table), Dolly Messiter, a matronly gossip, enters and recognizes Laura. Only then, as she accosts the couple, does the camera re-focus on them. Beyond their strange pensiveness, we are still not given any privileged information about them or their relationship. Dolly proceeds to dominate the conversation with her 'chattering and fussing,' until it is time for Alec to catch his train. His departure is marked by no more than a light touch of the hand on Laura's shoulder. While Dolly is asking for some chocolate, Laura disappears; a train is heard rushing by and, in a moment, she is standing alone in the doorway.

This same scene is played out a second time near the end of the film but from quite a different perspective – Laura's. Her memory now determines the narrative direction. Accordingly, Lean opens immediately

42

on the lovers in medium close two-shot at the corner table. Everything which had dominated the earlier rendering is now unimportant; the camera centers, intimately, on Laura and Alec.

> LAURA: You think we shall ever see each other again?
>
> ALEC: I don't know. Not for years, anyway.
>
> LAURA: The children will all be grown up. Wonder if we'll ever meet and know each other.
>
> ALEC: Couldn't I write to you, just once in a while?
>
> LAURA: No, Alec, please. You know we promised.
>
> ALEC: Oh, my dear, I do love you. So very much. I love you with all my heart and soul.
>
> LAURA: I want to die . . . if only I could die.
>
> ALEC: If you died, you'd forget me. I want to be remembered.
>
> LAURA: Yes, I know, I do too.
>
> ALEC: We've still got a few minutes.

At that moment Dolly interrupts the lovers (her disruptive appearance precipitates a cut as she literally forces her way into frame), but this time Laura's interior monologue and Rachmaninoff's music dominate the track. Her presence, her state of mind, alter the visualization of the event as well. The framing now focuses on Laura; the fill light goes down around her during her voice-overs. The departure bell rings; Alec prepares to leave:

> Laura: I felt the touch of his hand on my
> shoulder for a moment. And then he walked
> away . . . away out of my life forever . . . .
>
> Dolly still went on talking, but I wasn't
> listening to her. I was listening to the sound of
> his train starting. And it did. I said to myself 'He
> didn't go. At the last minute his courage failed
> him he couldn't have gone. Any minute now
> he'll come back into the refreshment room pre-
> tending he's forgotten something.' I prayed for
> him to do that . . . just so that I could see him
> again, for an instant. (pause) But the minutes
> went by.

'Poor, well meaning, irritating' Dolly again asks for chocolate, but this time she walks out of frame as we stay with Laura. The sound of an approaching train increases in volume and the camera travels in towards her. Abruptly it tilts: suddenly unbalanced, she jumps up and rushes out. A close shot catches her on the edge of the platform – wind blowing back her hair, and the light from the passing cars streaking across her face, pulsing like waves of mental anguish:

> LAURA: I meant to do it, . . . I really meant to do
> it. I stood there trembling right on the
> edge . . . but I couldn't

The sudden madness which began with her innocently 'extravagant' decision to purchase an expensive gift for her husband nearly culminates in death.

There are many other varied instances of intricate subjectification. After one of their Thursday rendezvous', for example, Laura within her own flashback imagines herself with Alec in various exotic locations. The countryside, as seen from her moving train, fades away and a series of fantasies are superimposed (dancing to a waltz; at the opera in Paris; on

Brief Encounter

elia Johnson as Laura in *Brief Encounter*

Above: Trevor Howard as Doctor Alec Harvey takes speck out of Laura's (Celia Johnson) eye

Left: Laura (Celia Johnson) and Dolly (Everley Gregg) in the station tea room.

above: Celia Johnson and Trevor Howard on the cold railway platform

below: Celia Johnson and Trevor Howard separated by the train

the Grand Canal in Venice; on a luxury liner; and beneath the palms of a tropical island). Each expresses Laura's desire to escape her unexciting existence and live out these schoolgirl daydreams. Soon, however, these images dissolve back into the dull English countryside, just as her transient love affair will fade. The scene in the refreshment room following Laura and Alec's first kiss is another type of subjective within subjective. When she recalls still within her flashback – half remorseful, half-glad – Alec's subtle invitation to go to his friend's unoccupied flat and her guarded refusal, we are not only dealing with Laura's memories but with her memories of memories.

Lean structures many of his films as series of oppositions, often favoring the contrasts of reality and dreams, of the unremarkable and the exceptional. Because most of the incidents in *Brief Encounter*'s love affair are seen through Laura's eyes (i.e. as she remembers them), we are necessarily subject to her interpretation of events and consequently must deal with her personality. Seen superficially, she is a sedate, stereotyped English matron – devoted to her family, largely unemotional, and exclusively concerned with the mundane matters of daily living (witness Alec's wry observation: 'What exciting lives we lead . . .'). This is the surface Laura Jesson. But her weekly excursions into town to shop, to go to the library, and see a movie unveil another side of Laura. Watching her during these separations from her family, one begins to sense that she is in search of something which her dull husband and monotonous home life do not offer. It may be found in a book of poetry (Fred: 'You're a poetry addict . . .'), or in a movie theater (where one can, on the screen, vicariously burn with *Flames Of Passion*), or even in the train station (where she first meets Alec). The restrictions on Laura are imposed by a world that frowns on the vicarious and impractical. Like the chain that prevents the passage of the rowboat, these are artificial but strongly forged. Lean dissolves from a medium long shot of the couple outside the theater to one of them in the park, an optical device that reduces the movement and dichotomy of the entire film. (Similarly, one might note the small credit beneath the glaring main title for *Flames of Passion*, 'based on the novel *Gentle Summer.').* For Laura exists on the brink of life where it takes no more than a chance cinder in her eye to ignite those flames of passion, to displace her customary sublimations. She begins to imagine, to dream, to love, and to agonize.

Laura's moments with Alec are polarized between 'unreflecting love' and disconsolate guilt, between elation and melancholy (a polarity made clear directly, in the dialogue, and reinforced by unconscious reactions, as in the case of the lady cellist/organist who changes from being funny to seeming sad). All of this affects Laura's memory of the affair. Through her perceptions a dreamlike Romanticism imbues the otherwise staid events. For although Alec and Laura never become lovers in the physical sense, part of the value of their passion is in the subjective transformation of their environment, in their escape from the drab material world into sensation. Rachmaninoff's wistful second piano concerto is played over scene as an equivalent to the lovers' emotions and as a contrast to the dismal visual reality of 'ordinary' concerns. As a narrative device it is justified when Laura herself 'chooses' it herself by switching on the radio after returning from her final parting with Alec. And Laura might well define her simple, middle class notion of love as 'hearing beautiful music all the time.' So, within the context of her recollection, is it appropriately present on the track.

*　　*　　*　　*　　*

As with most dreamers, the intrusions of society and its morality ultimately prove too constricting. Laura and Alec cannot 'let the great big world keep turning' (the song a barrel organ plays on the high street) and go about their own mad love. For that 'madness' (a word which Lean will use again and again to characterize his heroes and heroines, and which is situated in Fred's crossword puzzle between 'delirium' and 'Baluchistan') is too extreme. Laura is enmeshed in society's orderly puzzle – it clings vaguely to her and will not even let her yield to self-destructive impulses:

49

LAURA: I couldn't. I wasn't brave enough. I
should like to be able to say it was the thought
of you (Fred) and the children that prevented
me, but it wasn't. I had no thoughts at all.
Only an overwhelming desire not to feel
anything ever again.

The final sequence of the movie begins with a jump cut from Laura
standing in the doorway of the tea room to the frame of the story – Laura
sitting in the study with her husband. She looks disorientedly at Fred, as
if the abrupt change of scene had jarred her, rudely, awake.

FRED: Laura. (kneeling by her)

LAURA: Yes, dear.

FRED: Whatever your dream was, it wasn't a
very happy one, was it?

LAURA: No.

FRED: Is there anything I can do to help?

LAURA: Yes, Fred, you're always a help.

FRED: You've been a long way away. Thank
you for coming back to me. (Laura weeps).

Lean's most important characters are poised between this ephemeral
self-made fanciful universe and the safer, more solid, everyday world.
Laura yearns for the magic of the former but is tied by convention, by her
own insecurity, to the latter. Her life with Alec is symbolized by windy
excursions in a borrowed convertible and by the trains which speed in
and out of their scenes together. The constant movement of these vehicles
is representative of the dynamic yet unstable relationship Alec and Laura
have, while the solid, wood furniture and gray fixtures of Laura's house
symbolizes her 'normal' domestic life.

Laura's divergent attitude towards husband and lover is graphically expressed in one of the first scenes of the picture. When Laura begins her reverie, Lean uses a wide angle lens for her medium close shot suddenly forcing perspective, making the man and the objects in the room behind her literally farther away than they really are, visually rendering the interior state of mind which is drawing back from them into self. Lean extends this further by bringing down the key light on Fred and dissolving to the tea room, so that Laura remains visible in the foreground, 'watching' Alex enter and, on an imaginative level, visually substituting him for her husband (whom she literally fades out) without leaving her chair.

But this endistancing cannot be sustained; the natural strength she and Alec acquire in their wanderings is not sufficient to break habitual social ties. Laura's sad pronouncement, as she realizes her 'dream' is almost over is 'Nothing lasts really, neither happiness nor despair, not even life lasts very long.' Here she verbalizes the feeling of the entire tragic affair: smiles, furtive glances, brief moments of happiness, longer ones of anxiety – all end. Laura 'comes back' from the brink, fearful and resigned, to some obscure, pre-destined course of life, questioning as Wordsworth did:

> If this belief from heaven be sent,
> If such be Nature's holy plan,
> Have I not reason to lament
> What man has made of man?
>
> *(Lines Written in*
> *Early Spring)*

51

Chapter 3

The Dickens Adaptations

GREAT EXPECTATIONS (1946);

OLIVER TWIST (1948)

> The marshes were just a long black
> horizontal line then, as I stopped
> to look after him; and the river was
> just another horizontal line; and the
> sky was just a row of long angry red
> lines and dense black lines intermixed.

Charles Dickens, Great Expectations

EVEN BEFORE *Brief Encounter* was released, Lean was on location in 'Dickens country,' on the marshlands of East Kent along the Thames Estuary. Cineguild's new production took them, at last, into other source material than Coward's, but not fortunately into obscurity. In *Great Expectations* they chose one of the best-known and most popular novels in the language; and with this film Lean not only moves substantially out of the studio and modern settings into a period atmosphere, but also into a more socially-conscious context. That is not to say back into the overt wartime propaganda of *In Which We Serve,* but rather towards certain socio-critical elements discerned by James Agee and Raymond Durgnat in

53

Great Expectations, towards what the latter calls 'accidental Marxism.' Certainly, the bulk of that can be ascribed to Dickens, for *Great Expectations* is not only one of his most pessimistic works, on personal and character levels, but in its depictions of inflexible social convention and suffocating class structures, it seems to allow little chance for reform within the system. Dickens is less theoretically anti-capitalist than practically anti-industrialist, re-acting against an economic revolution perfidious for both the obvious evils of sweatshops, poorhouses, and child labour and for the implicit damage done to the human spirit by its cutthroat competitiveness. Jaggers, the self-made Nineteenth century man, and Wemmick, the clerk with the 'post-office mouth,' are serious and comic examples of the time's dehumanizing effects. But Dickens' abhorrence of mechanization is a state of mind and not a statement of particulars in fictional guise, is read not in passages of oratory but in patterns of images; and only in this latent form is it present in the film.

It could be said that Lean retains the character of the novel while making subtle changes in Dickens' hero, Philip Pirrip known as 'Pip.' For while both may concentrate thematically on the conflicts of an individual in and at least partially against society, Dickens' established method of placing an ordinary man in unusual circumstances does not correspond with Lean's emerging one of discovering a man (or woman) with a sense of the extraordinary trapped in a commonplace situation. Lean makes Pip more dynamic (but not on the scale of his later characterizations). More importantly, while he defines basically the same Pip as Dickens did, in translating the central images, Lean manages to do it in what might be called his own terms.

Pantheism. In adapting Dickens' animated universe, Lean makes more use of black-and-white exteriors than in any of his subsequent period films. The opening scene faithfully renders a contrast of dark stretches of earth and clouds against white sky. But Lean adds, silhouetted and dwarfed in extreme long shot, the figure of a boy. Pip is immediately caught in a tangle of pantheistic forces. He runs, and a pan follows him horizontally, as if driven by the natural lines of the landscape. Concurrently, his

54

vertical form is in opposition to that line. Finally, the pan reveals two gibbets: the first, in the distance, seems simply to impend doom (which for Pip is the imminent manifestation of Magwitch); the second, intruding into the right foreground of the frame, is more obviously a man-made object which graphically ruptures the natural pattern. By altering Dickens – Pip rather than Magwitch is the figure in the landscape; the background appears to propel him forward rather than trying 'to get a twist upon his ankle' – Lean rapidly establishes the figurative tug of natural versus artificial impulses on Pip. But he retains the tropistic distinctions between the boy and the convict. After the ominous low angles of Pip against the headstones in the graveyard and the wind rustling through tendrils and bare branches, Magwitch is suddenly before him as if sprung from the earth (his interruption of a panning shot is a geometric association which parallels Dickens' [the other of the] black things in all the prospect that seemed to be standing upright [was] a gibbet, with some chains hanging to it which had once held a pirate. The man was limping on towards this latter as if he were the pirate come to life, and come down, and going back to hook himself up again.'). Leaping out, posed with Pip against the hoary trees, Magwitch assumes a less human, hyper-natural dimension – the audience senses this *with* the character Pip at once, unlike the reader who must wait for the remarks of the narrator Pip at the end of the chapter.

In absolute terms, it is clear that the film Magwitch cannot possess all the facets of the novel's personnage. Instead of attempting to translate too much, Lean takes Dickens' 'animal imagery' and makes Magwitch an integral part of the animated, somewhat hostile surroundings. He arrives for the first time as a wind sweeps the cemetery; he is devoured by the shadows rowing back to the hulks after his recapture; and he re-appears at Pip's door in the midst of a storm. For the description of Magwitch which closes the first chapter, 'picking his way among the nettles' like a dark, lumbering beast, Lean substitutes the dynamic image of the struggle on the mud flats, in which Magwitch sinks into the marsh and literally becomes an extension of it. In the two-dimensions of the black-and-white frame Magwitch merges with the ground; in contrast, Pip and Joe, who stand watching this, are in sharp relief against the sky and distinctly detached from the natural elements within the slot.

Figurative Imagery. Many of the images in *Great Expectations* are carried over from Dickens. Pip's theft of the file and pie is a good example: His anxious voiceovers are taken from the text. 'The mist was heavier yet when I got out upon the marshes, so that instead of my running at everything, everything seemed to run at me' becomes a series of travelling shots through the fog. Even the imagined cries of 'Stop, thief' and 'Get up, Mrs. Joe' and the grazing cattle hurling accusations ('Halloa, young thief') are adapted (with the words superimposed over point-of-view medium close shots of the bull and cows). And, while the actual visualizations may not contain the wealth of linguistic colorations of the text, its subjective impressions are intensified – the 'Stop, thief' by its very disembodied presence on the track leaves the viewer startled by it as forcefully as the boy is and uncertain for an instant whether it is conjured up by Pip or really there.

Other usages seem less contrived on film. The sight of Jaggers washing his hands or of Wemmick casually dusting a deathmask with his coatsleeve are details which require individual comment for effect in novel form. In the movie, they become incidental bits of business covered by the scene's dialogue, more spontaneous and 'taken for granted (that is, as Pip is in the shot while Jaggers and Wemmick perform these actions, it is unnecessary for him to note them in an aside) and adding figurative value without being arbitrarily pointed out or underlined. Similarly, the impact of Pip's first sight of Miss Havisham, 'the strangest lady I have ever seen,' in the decaying splendour of Satis House – an event which requires several hundred words of description in the book – is instantaneous rather than cumulative. While items of decor in other scenes may also provide introductory character information (the print of a boxer on the wall of Herbert's lodgings reflecting his pugilistic aspirations; the glass-encased hangman's noose and even the severe arched doorway in Jagger's office capturing his Baroque business manner), they are unexpected, unemphatic, and inserted more for the viewer's casual notice than for Pip's. The entrance into Miss Havisham's domain, however, is a climax of dramatic anticipation – anticipation that is essentially Pip's. Dickens subjectifies his passage by stressing certain impressions ('white veil . . . dress . . . shoes . . . . hair of white;' 'Half-packed . . . not quite finished . . . half arranged'). Lean constructs the room and its inhabitant from the same passage and photographs the cobwebbed corners, the trinkets on the dressing table, all the various contents, in point-of-view. From the beginning, with the camera peering over Pip's shoulder at eye level while the door swings open gradually to reveal the inner sanctum, Lean stages in a way that draws the viewer into Pip's childish and apprehensive frame of reference.

Throughout, Lean not only adapts Dickens' literary tropes but derives and develops a variety of purely visual and/or original figurative concepts, contained within a single shot or extended over several sequences. For instance, when Jaggers enters the forge, there is a kind of synecdoche in the common film device of representing Joe and Pip by their shadows on the door. On a more elaborate level, Lean can relate, through a montage effect, a shot or arrows piercing a target back to Pip's fear of Estella's coldly precise behavior ('Will you always be part of Miss Havisham's plan?') or forward to the arrival of Bentley Drummle (three shots later) and, in so doing, can foreshadow both Pip's heart being pierced' and his despairing conversation with Estella at the ball ('You give him looks and smiles you never give me.' 'Do you want me then to deceive and entrap you?') – all wryly connected by the air of a stately dance on the soundtrack.

When Pip's hopes finally do expire and give way to the conflagration at Satis House, Lean – although he adheres to the specifics of Dickens' version of the occurrence – makes two key interpolations. First, he explicitly suggests that Havisham's death is ironically and inadvertently caused by Pip (in slamming the door behind him, he dislodges a piece of firewood which ignites her dress). Then, in ending with a high angle long shot of Pip kneeling by her body and collapsing by the 'great table,' stripped of its cloth and service and positioned on the right like a huge headstone, Lean implicitly erects a marker over the dissolution of Havisham's perverse existence and creates a metaphor for the entombment of Pip's 'great expectations' that simultaneously recalls their inception in the graveyard with Magwitch.

Lean also forges several links between Pip and the fixtures of the house. When he arrives 'to play,' a travelling shot back from the sunlit doorway reveals a black interior filling more and more of the frame, waiting to swallow him up like a crypt (which, indeed, is what its owner makes of it). Only Estella is key-lit inside, and it is she who calls him into the ominous darkness ('Don't loiter, boy'), who sets the mechanism of his fate in motion and leads him through the obscure passageways much as she will 'lead' him to become a gentleman. (There are also suggestions of the house as a womb – its insulated timelessness; the infantile aspects of Havisham's behavior – which Lean underscores when Pip leaves the house for the last time, superimposing his line, 'My boyhood has ended,' over an extreme long shot of him descending the stairs with Estella). Perhaps the most expressive sequence in the film is the escape down the river at night, the tiny skiff is lost among the hulls of the cargo ships (matte shots of miniatures); on the track the sounds of the vessels creaking at anchor mingle with the crewmen's songs and muffle the strokes of the oars. Suddenly a figurehead looms into the foreground of a high angle shot; over a reverse someone, unseen, cries, 'Ahoy, there.' The head itself looks down on them like the face of God, as if incarnating a placid destiny that witnesses their passage, voices a challenge, and lets them hold their course knowing where it will lead.

Irony, Subjectivity, and Comic Relief. The ship's figurehead also recalls the face of Compeyson, Magwitch's pursuer, as he follows Herbert out of the shipping office. That incident is one of only two that Lean records in the ironic mode, the other being the start of the fire. Both incidents complement the main thematic line: Havisham's death by relating, as previously noted, the end of Pip's false hopes in Miss Havisham (immediately preceding) back to the real cause of his 'expectations' (helping

58

Magwitch). Compeyson's face and the figurehead 'hang over' the vulnerable Magwitch, but unknown to Pip. The final ironic layer is that, in his ignorance, he causes or allows to perish (i.e. gets revenge against) both people who have fostered those deceptive and shallow expectations. This concept is peculiar to the adaptation, for in the novel Pip is neither responsible (except, by association, in his fantasy of her suicide) for Havisham's death nor as unaware of the imminence of the threat of Compeyson as in the film. By restricting the irony in this manner, Lean is more than faithful to the original's first person style; for, excepting these two brief moments (and one other, equally brief, when Mrs. Joe rides up to dispatch Pip to Satis House), the film, too, is in the first person – Pip is present in and party to *every* scene.

Within that overall narrative subjectivity, Lean obtains a number of particular effects. Pip's voiceovers throughout, the sequence with the cattle, entering Miss Havisham's room as already described, the first fascinating close shot of Estella through the house gate, the low angle of the grown-ups at the Christmas party – all are standard devices defining a specific point-of-view. On a less obvious level, a shot may, as in *Brief Encounter,* catch the inner state of a protagonist. In Pip's dialogue with Estella on the stairs, for example, his own sense of inferiority is reflected in the cross-cut over-shoulder shots which angle up towards her (a step above) and down towards him. To approximate Pip's tension in his first adult re-encounter with Estella, Lean follows them in a long, unbroken medium two-shot as they walk through the garden. To add to his discomfort, he is forced to awkwardly sidestep hanging vines and other vegetation. But the most complete externalization of sensation in *Great Expectations* is contained in Pip's collapse after Magwitch's death. Lean begins with a travelling medium close shot of Pip walking unsteadily down a crowded street. Gradually the oppressive whirr inside his brain leaks onto the soundtrack; a light spins dizzily and is superimposed over his face. Then the camera becomes Pip, lurching forward through his front door and into his room but falling short of the bed. His loss of consciousness becomes a cut to black (an effect repeated in *Oliver Twist*);

after a moment of silence and a dark screen, he 'comes to his senses' with a slow, blurry fade-in, focusing on a close shot of the ever effusive and egregious Joe Gargery.

Between the subjective and the comedic aspects of the original – as represented principally by Joe – Lean clearly concentrates on the former. That is not to say that the film is solemnly dramatic – Joe, Wemmick, and Herbert Pocket (both the 'young gentleman' throwing in the sponge and Alec Guinness' interpretation of the grown Herbert) retain the innate humor Dickens gave them. The more serious caricatures – Francis L. Sullivan as the portly Jaggers; Martita Hunt as the grotesque Havisham – are also aptly rendered.* But Lean uses comedy sparingly and with greater integration as the film progresses. The cart ride with Uncle Pumblychook where the music replaces the dialogue or the dinner with Herbert where Pip receives instruction in table manners ('In London it's not the custom to put the knife in the mouth – for fear of accident') advance the plot while providing comic relief but do nothing more. Later, Joe's visit to London, that concludes with his hat floating in Pip and Herbert's teapot, occasions some serious introspection by Pip, which Lean visually parallels in a mirror shot (with the accompanying figurative implication of a gilt frame around Pip in a rich dressing gown), so that the comedy provides a lead-in for Pip to strike one of the film's most thematically serious poses. The final bit of comedy is perhaps the most telling and least amusing: Pip's meeting with the Aged Parent. Wemmick by compelling Pip to nod and humor his senile father before he will pass on the information about Magwitch, frustrates both Pip ('I am anxious to know what happened') and the viewer, who by identification and purely as one following the plot is equally anxious to know. By altering the circumstances of his first visit to Wemmick's home at Walworth [it

---

* In fact, the only real problem in *Great Expectations* is that John Mills' adult Pip, but for a few lighter moments (posing proudly in his new, out-of-fashion suit; adding up debts with Herbert; the montage of becoming a gentleman) fluctuates too sharply between boyish enthusiasm and forlorn brooding; and the middle third of the picture with its rapid episodes seems slightly out of pace with Pip's boyhood (first third) and the events after Magwitch's return (last third).

reat Expectations

(Anthony Wager), as a child, in the graveyard in *Great Expectations*.

Above: Pip (Anthony Wager).

Left: Young Pip (Antho... Wager) with Miss Havis... (Martita Hunt).

Opposite: The grown-u... (John Mills) and the ni... porter.

Above: ''I had become a snob.'' Pip (John Mills) sees himself in the mirror after Joe's visit.

Below: The return of Magwitch (Finlay Currie) to Pip (John Mills).

should be noted that an earlier scene there is included in the final shooting script but was cut from the picture), Lean also alters the thrust of Dickens' comedy. For the Aged Parent, in his original context, would probably seem extraneous and can only be justifiably carried over as a foil to manipulate the audience into sharing Pip's emotion and heighten rather than relieve the dramatic suspense.

The Ending. There were two conclusions to *Great Expectations* written by Dickens;* the film provides a third. Like Dickens' revised version (which, unless otherwise noted, will be the only one considered from here on), it is ostensibly a 'happy ending' in which the novel's final 'broad expanse of tranquil light [in which] I saw no shadow of another parting from her' is translated into a long shot of Pip and Estella closing the gate of Satis House behind them, locking out the past while the sentiment of the title is re-affirmed (by being superimposed in large letters over the shot). It seems an image of abundant hope and appropriately so, fulfilling the demands of an essentially melodramatic story in a pleasing, slightly tearful, joyful, superficial, and generally satisfying manner. But, still following Dickens, it leaves several deeper implications unresolved.

To begin with, the screenplay extensively elaborates on both the narrative and psychological lines of the novel. Dickens sets the last meeting in what has been critically dubbed a 'ruined garden' (' . . . no house now, no brewery, no building whatever left, but the wall of the old garden.') – in the film, Pip slowly walks through the still extant house up to Miss Havisham's room, recalling as he does earlier visits (with accompanying voiceovers from past encounters at the gate, on the stairs, and along the darkened corridors). He discovers Estella upstairs; and for the first time in the picture the dialogue and the whole thrust of the scene radically diverge from the original:

* Dickens' pessimistic ending in which Pip and his godson speak briefly with Estella (widowed and remarried) takes place in London and is, in novel time, two years later than the revision (which was produced at the urging of Edward Bulwer-Lytton before the original serial publication in 1860).

[NOVEL]

PIP: (seeing her on the garden walk)
Estella!

ESTELLA:
I am greatly changed. I wonder you know me.

[They sit on a bench]

PIP:
After so many years, it is strange that we should meet thus again, Estella, here where our first meeting was! Do you often come back?

ESTELLA:
I have never come here since.

PIP:
Nor I.

[The moon begins to rise]

ESTELLA: (crying)
I have very often hoped and intended to come back but have been prevented by many circumstances. Poor, poor old place! Were you wondering, as you walked along how it came to be left in this condition?

PIP:
Yes, Estella.

[FILM]

M.S. PIP entering the room
ESTELLA'S VOICE:
Pip.

M.L.S. ESTELLA (POV) by the dressing table.

M.S. PIP
PIP:
Estella.

L.S. PIP over Estella's shoulder
PIP: (walking towards her)
What are you doing here? I thought you were in Paris with your husband.

M.C.S. ESTELLA over Pip
ESTELLA:
I have no husband, Pip. Have you not heard?

PIP:
I have been ill, Estella. I have heard nothing.

ESTELLA:
When Mr. Jaggers disclosed to Bentley Drummle my true parentage . . . (looking down) . . . he no longer wished to have me for a wife.

ESTELLA:
The grounds belong to me. It is
the only possession I have not
relinquished. Everything else has
gone from me, little by little, but
I have kept this. It was the
subject of the only determined
resistance I made in all the
wretched years.

PIP:
Is it to be built on?

ESTELLA:
At last it is, I came here to take
leave of it before its change. And
you, you live abroad still?

PIP:
Still.

ESTELLA:
And do well, I am sure.

PIP:
I work pretty hard for a
sufficient living, and therefore –
Yes, I do well!

ESTELLA:
I have often thought of you.

PIP:
Have you?

M.C.S. PIP over Estella
ESTELLA:
Well, Pip. Why don't you
laugh? You have every right.

PIP:
I've no wish to laugh, Estella.
I'm truly sorry.

M.C.S. ESTELLA over Pip
ESTELLA:
You've no need to pity me. It
simplifies my life.

M.C.S. PIP over Estella
ESTELLA:
There is no need to sell the
house. It is mine and I shall live
here.

[She sits down. Music]

M.S. ESTELLA in Miss
Havisham's chair
ESTELLA:
I shall like it here, Pip, Away
from the world and all its
complications.

C.S. PIP looking at Estella, then
to the right.

C.S. THE DRESSING TABLE
(POV) a new pair of white
gloves, a prayer book, and pearls
which were for Estella's
wedding.

67

ESTELLA:
Of late very often. There was a
long hard time when I kept far
from me the remembrance of
what I had thrown away when I
was quite ignorant of its worth.
But since my duty has not been
incompatible with the admission
of the remembrance, I have
given it a place in my heart.

PIP:
You have always held your place
in *my* heart.

ESTELLA:
I little thought that I should
take leave of you in taking leave
of this spot. I am very glad to
do so.

PIP:
Glad to part again, Estella. To
me, parting is a painful thing.
To me the remembrance of our
last parting has been ever
mournful and painful.

M.S. ESTELLA seated left and
PIP standing over her on
CAMERA RIGHT

PIP: (gravely)
How long have you been here,
Estella?

ESTELLA:
I don't know.

PIP: (moving closer)
Estella, you must leave this
house. It's a dead house.
Nothing can live here. Leave it,
Estella, I beg of you.

ESTELLA:
What do you mean? This is the
house where I grew up. It's part
of me. It's my home.

PIP:
It's Miss Havisham's home. But
she's gone, Estella. Gone from
this house, from you, from both
of us.

ESTELLA:
She is not gone. She is still here
with me, in this house, in this
very room.

PIP:
Then I defy her.

68

ESTELLA:

But you said to me, 'God bless you, God forgive you!' And if you could say that to me then, you will not hesitate to say that to me now – now when suffering has been stronger than all other, and has taught me to understand what your heart used to be. I have been bent and broken, but – I hope – into a better shape. Be as considerate and good to me as you were, and tell me we are friends.

PIP: (standing)
We are friends.

ESTELLA:
And will continue friends apart.

['I took her hand in mine, and we went out of the ruined place; and as the morning mists had risen long ago when I first left the forge, so the evening mists were rising now, and in all the broad expanse of tranquil light they showed to me, I saw no shadow of another parting from her.']

M.S. PIP in the middle of the room.

PIP: (shouting)
I have come back, Miss Havisham.

L.S. PIP. Estella remains in the chair
PIP:
I have come back to let in the sunlight.

M.C.S. PIP tears down a curtain

M.S. ESTELLA suddenly backlit.

L.S. PIP tearing down more curtains

M.S. ESTELLA as light strikes her face

L.S. ESTELLA looks up. Pip stands behind among the crumpled draperies
PIP:
Look, Estella, look. Nothing but dust and decay.

M.C.S. PIP walks back to Estella
PIP: (bending over)
I have never ceased to love you even when there seemed no hope for my love. You are part of my existence, part of myself, Estella. Come with me. Out into the sunlight.

69

[She stands. He catches her
by the shoulders]

M.S.2S. PIP and ESTELLA
PIP:
Look at me.

ESTELLA: (looking away)
Pip. I'm afraid.

PIP:
Look at me.

[She turns slowly towards him]
PIP:
We belong to each other. Let's
start again. Together.

ESTELLA: (half-laughing,
half-sobbing) Oh, Pip.

MUSIC swells.   DISSOLVE TO:

*M.L.S. CORRIDOR OF SATIS
HOUSE* as Pip and Estella run
out. They turn to look back at
the gate.

GREAT
EXPECTATIONS

is superimposed over shot as they
go out into the sunlight.

Both scenes are verbally explicit, but Dickens' is more overtly directed
towards filling in character exposition (explaining what has happened
emotionally, particularly to Estella–, ... suffering has been stronger than
all other, and has taught me to understand what your heart used to be.'

– in the intervening years) and ends with only a possibility of re-con-
ciliation not a *fait accompli*. The talk is not exactly mundane (although
Pip's remarks on his career approach it) but swathed in rhetorical ('!')
gentility. Pip plays an observational role (noting the vegetation, the
moon, the morning mists) and remains conversationally passive, allowing
Estella to lead him. In the film, the emphasis shifts to Pip: *he* directs the
scene towards its climax. Moreover, as the dialogue is less rhetorical and
the exchange more spontaneous and enlivened, a markedly less composed
Estella emerges. She is still proud, much nearer arrogance than in
Dickens, but, within the sequence itself, she grows more distant and
distracted and finally, it becomes apparent, is on the verge of
schizophrenic withdrawal. This metamorphosis into a second Miss
Havisham is well outside the scope of Dickens' conception; but it does
follow from the underlying notion of Estella having been bred by
Havisham to 'wreak revenge on the male sex.' Being conditioned to
patterned responses, Estella herself gives the reason for her breakdown –
a deviation from the pattern: Drummle's rejection. That rejection
(Dickens does not mention it or, for that matter, Drummle at all,
although in the original ending he died fittingly enough 'from an
accident consequent on ill-treating a horse') also recreates the chief
circumstances of and motivation for Miss Havisham's retreat from the
exterior world.

From the opening lines Dickens almost stresses the fortuitous coincidence of the encounter, clearly establishing that both have chosen the
same day to return for the first time after lengthy absences. Perhaps,
speculating from the knowledge that he was in the process of an alteration and not working from the first light of inspiration, it could be
argued that Dickens was anticipating and trying to undercut potential
criticism of that coincidence as far-fetched; and, indeed, it seems so. In
any case, Lean does not have to grapple with that problem in its literary
context; and he understates the chance quality of their meeting. Again he
uses identification with the 'first person' Pip to manipulate audience
response: in Pip's preceding tour of the house, Lean restricts observable

reality to what *he* sees and hears. When Pip enters the upstairs room, the first suggestion of Estella's presence is her over shot exclamation of his name; the first shot of her is a point-of-view. The sudden fact of her being in the room and the surprise of it shared with Pip allow no time for speculation on how she came to be there or the relative likelihood of it – disbelief stays suspended by her very material presence and by the mutual need of Pip and the audience to make an immediate response to it.

This Estella lurking in the corners of Satis House is substantially different from Dickens'. Sitting amid the ruins, his heroine is pensive, even nostalgic, but still logical and keenly aware of her position (of not just the physical surroundings but the emotional terrain as well). Dickens gives her not only the bulk of the dialogue with four complete short speeches but also the key lines which provide most of the narrative information; Lean defines Estella's new compulsion objectively: she arranges her things on a dressing table and sits stiffly before them in the same way Miss Havisham did. And the viewer shares the perception with Pip, for he is the distinguishing factor between the two women. As a doting lover he gave Havisham satisfaction in being something *she* could not have (and her failure to form a direct relationship with Pip, her emotional inability to be his or anyone's benefactoress, exacts its toll in his physical inability to save her from the fire), while re-inforcing rather than undermining Estella's aloofness. But he *can* save her, by replacing the lost suitor and by taking advantage of what is, for the first time her inferior position (a position Lean underscores in his staging, beginning with cross-cut medium close shots in which Pip and Estella are 'equal' then shooting from behind her, up at Pip who stands while she sits, so that he no longer appears to be shorter than she is). Dickens' Pip is still somewhat immature, uncertain at best, still timidly resigned at worst to waiting for direction, a perpetual parody of the industrious Herbert Pocket's 'looking about' him. The 'ruined garden' becomes an image of a new beginning both through its archetypal associations with Eden and in its resemblance to the graveyard of the opening chapter. But Lean uses

72

Oliver Twist

gin (Alec Guinness) threatens to murder Oliver Twist (John Howard Davies) because the boy has seen
m gloating over his stolen treasures. A scene from *Oliver Twist*.

Above: Mr Bumble, the Beadle, played by Francis L. Sullivan.

Below: The Parish board in session in *Oliver Twist.* Ivor Barnard, chairman, is seen standing.

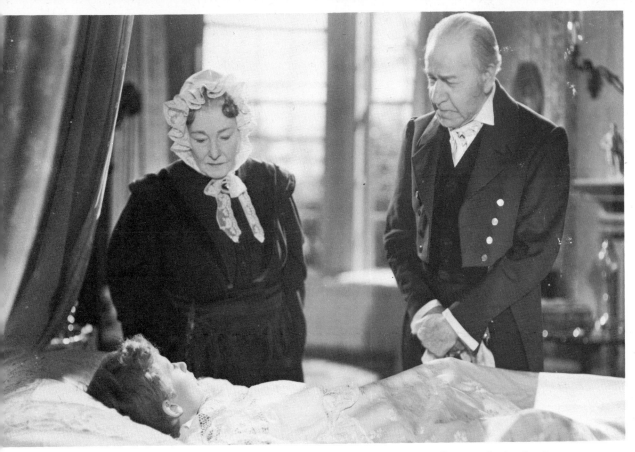

above: Mr. Brownlow (Henry Stephenson) and Mrs. Bedwin (Amy Veness) try to discover facts about Oliver's (John Howard Davies) life in London.

below: Robert Newton, as Bill Sikes, subdues Kay Walsh (Nancy) after she has railed against Fagin.

each visit to Satis House as a gauge of Pip's adulthood – his docility as a child, his hurt, adolescent anger in the last confrontation with Havisham, and finally, in this scene, his maturity in handling Estella.

The central figurative image in Pip's action, although it may have been suggested by Dickens' tone or by his 'tranquil light,' is also original to the film. Estella does not respond to his arguments, so Pip illuminates the situation by tearing down the curtains and literally 'let[ting] in the sunlight.' In a series of three cuts, Lean adds backlight and sidelight to a low-key medium shot of Estella in Havisham's chair: her re-action is stylized – startled, dazed, looking around in wonderment as Pip exposes the 'dust and decay.' Figuratively, by allowing time, even in the primitive movement of suncast shadows across the floor, to re-enter Satis House, Miss Havisham's spell is broken. For just as Lean can forego Dickens' verbal expressions of astonishment at the chance meeting in favor of equally explicit re-action shots from his actors, he can resolve the plotted psychological conflicts on a purely graphic level. In this, the ending is non-realist – part of a scheme where figurative meanings become primary events. For even without the implication of reversal of Pip's earlier entry into the dark house as a child, the final image of Pip and Estella passing through the front door 'out into the sunlight' still achieves its major, narrative purpose. But without the arrangement of shots to delineate the truly metaphysical effect of the light on Estella, she cannot be transformed, cannot be deterred from mental self-destruction.

In his closing chapter, Dickens sets in motion a cycle of regression on Pip's part. As if longing for the lost innocence of youth, for the period before his disillusionment, the narrator Pip accelerates the passage of time (eleven years go by in a single sentence) and rushes towards old age and a 'second childhood.' In his namesake (Joe and Biddy's son who is never conceived in the film) the young Pip of the novel's beginning re-appears. Lean forges his own link with Pip's childhood through Satis House, as previously noted, and more specifically with a single medium close shot of the grown Pip reclining on a slope and tugging at the grass in exactly the same position he assumed as a boy when Estella first caused his dissatisfaction. Visually Pip returns to the moment when he only dreamed of being a gentleman; now, having been made so by Magwitch, he nevertheless verbally concedes that 'that poor dream has all gone by . . . all gone by.' That point in the novel is, as it happens, where Dickens begins his revision. In the film, that shot in its recollection and synthesis of a past time with a stated present realization marks the instant where Lean moves beyond the book and records the completion of Pip's maturation.

That occurrence, more than anything else, also makes plausible as well as possible the 'happy' ending. 'Happy,' in quotes, because just as Dickens subjectively speeds up his character's regressive desires, Lean carefully outlines the frame of reference in his conclusion. The voiceovers as Pip wanders through the house are all of the young Estella and demonstrate a lingering fascination with the past. Accordingly, when the real Estella calls his name, it is initially unclear whether she is actually there or merely another imagined voice. Even the point-of-view shot of her is ambiguous: one of the film's most pictorially lustrous, almost a portrait, almost too stylishly lit and perfectly composed to be anything but a vision or a dream.

Obviously this line of analysis can lead, not unreasonably, to an interpretation of the ending as a complex fantasy created by Pip and culminating in the unreal, transcendent slow motion as the couple run ('float' would be more accurate) hand in hand from the house. Even as reality, there are several limitations (for example, in the last shot inside Havisham's room, the camera sees Estella in profile and Pip has a full-face view – only he is literally in a position to judge the genuineness of her expression when she says, 'Oh, Pip;' and he is not above self-deception) and disturbing touches (the fact that the concluding shots build in a way that is roughly analogous, right down to the surge of exultant music, to the wait for the packet boat which ended in crushed hopes; or the latent irony in the superimposed 'Great Expectations:' the future may be only that and nothing more. Many questions are never resolved. The ending achieves a certain degree of interaction and fulfills several functions within itself; but much as the novel's vague 'shadow of another parting' does not entirely lift, traces of ambiguity linger over the film as a whole.

* * * * *

Oliver cried lustily. If he could have
known that he was an orphan, left to the
tender mercies of church-wardens and
overseers, perhaps he would have cried
the louder.

Charles Dickens

Lean's second and final Dickens adaptation was *Oliver Twist*. An early novel, it has the same humor and sentiment as *Great Expectations* but lacks the polish and cohesion of Dickens' later work. Moreover, it tends to dwell more overtly on images of social injustice and sordid criminality. The early scenes in the parish workhouse bear this out.

In this sequence, Lean creates a series of ironic contrasts drawn directly from Dickens' detailed, atmospheric descriptions of this establishment. A light-hearted interlude between the Beadle (Mr. Bumble) and the Matron is positioned among the scenes of human exploitation and maltreatment. The Parish Board's pronouncement of 'this workhouse has become a regular place of entertainment for the poorer classes' is met by a decisive cut to women slaving over wash tubs. A scene of house officials enjoying an opulent feast is juxtaposed with images of Oliver and the half-starved orphans, 'voracious and wild with hunger' as Dickens described them. Finally, huge, sermonizing carvings proclaiming that 'God is Love' loom over the heads of downtrodden scrubwomen. In Lean's hands, the film becomes as effective an indictment of Victorian society as its 1837 source.

Oliver's final release from this 'dreadful place' leads him first to the home of a mortician, where he is abused and beaten, and then to bustling, impersonal London, where he is adopted by a gang of thieves. Fagin (the leader of the young pickpockets) and his 'charges' are, at first glance, rather humorous characters – treating Oliver to a much-needed meal and a laugh. But as their situation worsens and Oliver becomes a threat to them, they are not above kidnapping him from his newly-found grand-father and imprisoning him in their hideout. The figure who best represents this world which Oliver has fallen into with its degradation, criminality, and vice, is Bill Sikes. Lean, like Dickens, refuses to glamorize this outlaw, his cohorts, or his society. With Sikes, in par-ticular, there is a strong temptation to transform the caricature of evil drawn by Dickens into a misunderstood, semi-tragic misfit. But the adaptors resist this impulse; and Sikes remains simply a thief and mur-derer who commits the 'unforgivable act' – killing the one who loves him. His complete lack of scruples or conscience (whether in beating a child or trying to drown his own dog) lead him, by the final reel, to become more a wild beast than a human being – an animal pursued by an angry mob until he is cornered and lashes out in terror. At no time during this chase nor in any other scene is the audience asked to em-pathize with Sikes. He is an archetypal villain whose ugly death at the end of a rope seems eminently just.

The only person in this brood of greedy scoundrels who captures sympathy, no matter how briefly, is the pathetic Nancy. For the conno-tations of frail flowers on her dresser, her inexplicable love for Sikes, and her maternal affection for Oliver betray a sensitive nature which is usually hidden beneath a cynical facade. The scene in which she first elicits involvement comes after she and Sikes have recaptured Oliver. Beginning to entertain second thoughts about exploiting the boy, she delivers a revealing verbal attack against Fagin:

> NANCY:
> 'Civil words, civil words,' you villain. Yes, you
> deserve 'em from me. I thieved for you when I
> was a child not half his [Oliver's] age. And
> I've thieved for you ever since, don't you
> know it.
>
> FAGIN:
> And if you have, it is your living.

79

NANCY:

Aye, it is. It is my living. And the cold, wet, dirty streets are my home. And you're the wretch that drove me to them long ago. And that'll keep me there . . .

> (As she becomes more hysterical the *camera tilts* to visualize her frenzy)

Day and night, till I die!

Dickens, however, for all his impassioned outcries of social injustice, was too much a product of his age to carry his protests to the extremes of a Marx. As with *Great Expectations,* the times demanded that he end his tale on a sentimental and rosy note; and he did. Further, he even managed to exonerate much of Victorian England very neatly in the person of Mr. Brownlow, Oliver's grandfather. He is the principal agent of destruction for the Fagin-Sikes-Monks ring. In bringing the insidious Monks to justice and in demoting the workhouse tyrant, Mr. Bumble, the members of Victorian society could identify with this avenging angel and, thereby, relieve whatever guilt they may have had. It would take many years and many more novels before Dickens was to question, in *Great Expectations,* this optimism and find it wanting.

*　　*　　*　　*　　*

Lean's first task in his adaptations of novels has always been one of condensation. Obviously, in terms of the practical limits of screen time, an attempt to transfer a novel intact could be rather foolhardy (evidence Von Stroheim's *Greed*). The art of condensing, then, is in knowing what to keep and what to discard, while maintaining the 'sense' of the original. According to Bazin 'a good adaptation should result in a restoration of the essense of the letter and the spirit.'

Lean's rendering of the dark, almost claustrophobic mood of the book is masterful. The dreary workhouse, the morbid atmosphere of the mortician's shop (where Oliver sleeps among the coffins, as in the novel), the filth of Fagin's hideout, and the decadence of the society around the Two Boars Inn are all photographed in low-key, with meticulous attention to recreating the locales as Dickens saw them. The only exceptions to this oppressive background are, appropriately, the scenes at Mr. Brownlow's home. Oliver's light-filled bedroom and the final shot of the house with the three happy figures (Oliver, Mr. Brownlow, and the servant, Mrs. Bedwin) framed in front of the glaring whiteness of its exterior act as a definite counterpoint to the general grimness of the film's decor. For inside Oliver has escaped the unfriendly society around him and found refuge in his grandfather's love.

The most direct visualizations of Dickens' words are in the imaginative characterizations. The author's caricatures come to life in *Oliver Twist* as they had in *Great Expectations.* The Beadle, exactly as Dickens conjured him up, is a 'fat man, and a choleric.' His pretensions to dignity and genteel language are as humorous on film as they were in print. Noah Claypole is 'a large-headed, small-eyed youth, of lumbering make.' And Fagin, as interpreted by Alec Guinness, co-incides perfectly with the greedy but comic original – 'a very old shrivelled Jew, whose villainous-looking and repulsive face was obscured by a quantity of red hair. He was dressed in a greasy flannel gown, with his throat bare.'*

Most probably the greatest problem in paring down the novel was the jumbled plot. With even more assurance than in *Great Expectations,* Lean had to select which elements to retain and which to eliminate. Consequently the contrived meanderings of the original became, in the film, a few, much simpler plot twists. The Monks character, originally a rather involved and melodramatic figure who continually popped up like a bad penny, appears in very few of the movie's scenes and then only as a

---

* The make-up was modelled after engravings by Cruikshank, complete with beak nose. Considerable controversy was aroused over the alleged anti-Semitism of this characterization. In Germany, there were riots at the opening. In the United States pressure from the Jewish Anti-defamation League caused the film to be repeatedly denied an MPAA Seal of Approval. Finally after several cuts were made, primarily in comic episodes involving Fagin, the film received its U.S. premiere almost three years after its British release.

narrative-furthering *deus ex machina* or, alternately, as a symbol of evil. The benevolent Rose and Harry – like Monks related in some obscure way to Oliver – are dropped. In their place Lean combines all the 'do-gooders' into one, the person of Mr. Brownlow. The eloquent diction of the child Oliver is replaced by a speech more natural to someone his age. Finally, Lean exploits the inherent condensing quality of the image. In a few seconds, with a minimum of shots, Lean can 'say' what may have taken the visually-oriented Dickens pages to describe. Again the workhouse sequence is exemplary. While Dickens devotes four chapters to Oliver's abuse and misery in this place, Lean uses a montage of short scenes to convey all the drudgery, starvation, and regimentation. There is a characteristic ease with which Lean creates mood and atmosphere through montages like this one. But it would be a little too much to expect an artist as personal as Lean to completely submerge himself to Dickens. Traces of Lean's hand are frequently observable and the most striking instances are in the editing. Besides its aforementioned economy, there is its unerring precision. The final chase, in which a constantly enlarging crowd follows Sikes' dog to the murderer's hideout, is framed and cut to pace a steady increase in momentum. (As the dog and the mass of people rush, diagonally and dynamically, across the frame and through the London streets, the audience is caught up with them in the race to find Sikes). Lean's ironic and dialectical cutting is also on display. The juxtaposition of animals being herded through the London streets is intercut with shots of stifling crowds milling by. Equally ironic is the cut from Fagin assuring the Dodger that the spying will be 'a pleasant piece of work' to the miserable boy standing out in a rainstorm. There is one instance, however, where Lean is directly inspired by Dickens for his cutting. The author, within approximately fifteen sentences in the novel, describes the responses to Oliver's request for 'more food.' The writing leaps across space and time to accommodate rapid and humorous glimpses of the elders' reactions. Similarly, Lean moves in four cuts from the overseer, to the Beadle, to the Matron, and finally to the assembled Parish Board. On a number of levels, Dickens presages the motion picture in his writings – whether in minor instances such as this or in major ones such as the suspenseful intercutting across wide expanses of space in *A Tale of Two Cities,** providing inspiration for directors from Griffith to David Lean.

Like the book, Lean's *Oliver Twist* is not a first person narrative; but this does not prevent the adaptors from straying from the observer mode Dickens has established. There are several prominent examples: the pursuit of Oliver by an angry mob following the theft of Mr. Brownlow's 'wipe,' the subjective camera in the courtroom (both from the boy's point of view), and Sikes' hallucinations after Nancy's murder. All subtly but forcefully add another, more personal level to the film.

Although Dickens' original is almost completely confined to urban scenes, Lean adds a number of nature images. The opening storm is not found in the book. The initial sequence – as black storm clouds gather over a dark, windswept heath – are an original conception forming a kind of prologue to the parish workhouse scenes. The thunder and lightning which responds to her pain, the bending briars symbolizing her sorrow are animated on film in a way they could never be by Dickens. Moreover, the suggestions of interaction between the cosmos and human events in her ordeal are most typical of Lean. The flashes illuminate the sign on the workhouse gate; but concurrently the ditches in the ground cause her to stumble, the ominous, howling winds hold her back – both are constructs in Lean's dualistic view of a nature both beneficent and maleficent.

At some point in Lean's films his heroes or heroines must assert or defend their freedom of action. Oliver's moment comes when Noah defiles the memory of his [Oliver's] dead mother. He leaps at and pommels the defamer, only to be beaten in turn by Noah's re-inforcements. In a series of shots (which are repeated almost exactly in *Lawrence of Arabia* during Lawrence's torture by the Turks), Oliver is spread-eagled and whipped. Though the beating is severe, he refuses to

---

* Eisenstein even claims to have discovered a 'lap dissolve' in the second paragraph of this novel's final chapter.

wince or cry out, much to the consternation of Noah. For as Mrs. Sowerberry remarked earlier, 'He must be mad' – mad, indeed, with the exhilaration of independence.

Chapter 4

MADELEINE
(1950)

I know from experience that the world
is not lenient in its observations. But
I don't care for the world's remarks so
long as my own heart tells me I am doing
nothing wrong.

Letter from Madeleine
Smith to Pierre Emile
L'Angelier, 1855

Certainly these letters show as extraordinary a frame of mind and as unhal-
lowed a passion as perhaps ever appeared
in a Court of Justice.

John Hope, Lord Justice
Clerk at the trial of
Madeleine Smith, 1857

MADELEINE (1950) is Lean's most serious examination of Nineteenth
century Great Britain, deadly serious in both its subject matter and tone.

Almost devoid of comic relief, it deals with murder – not the compulsive, agonized killings of a misfit such as Bill Sikes – but murder of convenience, murder of a discarded lover planned and executed by a woman of twenty-one years fresh from a London finishing school.* Today the case of Madeleine Hamilton Smith itself may seem if not innocuous, certainly far from extraordinary in its characters and events. And yet the kind of contemporary notoriety it received, the solemn social judgments it engendered are typical of the formal hypocrisy that has come to be associated with mid-Victorianism, with the unconscious tug-of-war that pitted outward insistence on 'proper behavior' against the inward fascination of passion. If that passion was, in the public eye (and in a good many repressed, private ones) 'criminal' and those who corresponded with it fallen men and women, it is clear, too, in light of such studies as Marcus' *Other Victorians* (if not in the socio-economic history of the time) that sexual impulses were not different then, nor sexual transgression all that uncommon. It is equally clear that they were either kept secret or politely overlooked by a strange code of conduct that objected less to any given 'illicit' acts than to being compelled to the distasteful extreme of having to speak openly about them. Lean and his screenwriters were not out to judge Madeleine Smith – that had been accomplished a hundred years before – but rather to interpret her 'exceptional' story from this mid-Twentieth century perspective, to explain what the prologue calls 'an interest [in her] which time can never change.' Accordingly, *Madeleine* begins in an almost documentary style: a view of modern Glasgow, factory chimneys and white smoke, the low relief of two and three-storey grey brick houses, and 'in this great city of Glasgow there is a square. . Blytheswood Square ... there's nothing very remarkable about its appearance ...' As simply and unobtrusively as that, the picture's

---

* The film makes use not only of trial records but of Madeleine Smith's letter and Emile L'Angelier's memorandum book (not admitted as evidence) to follow the course of actual occurrences. There are several books on the case, most recently two editions of the *Notable British Trials* series, edited by A. Duncan Smith (1907) and F. Tennyson Jesse (1927) and *The Madeleine Smith Affair* by Peter Hunt (1950) which derived partly from research material assembled by the filmmakers.

underlying tension is introduced. For just as her city and her house are genuinely commonplace (then and, the images suggest, now), Madeleine Smith will prove an outwardly conventional, somewhat undistinguished young woman. The real question, the one that makes the whole drama possible, is why she should so startle the good citizens of Glasgow, should so arouse their prurient interest or incite their moral indignation. Why should the name of the well-bred, slightly spoiled, second daughter of a prosperous member of the Scottish gentry, a girl who quite possibly poisoned her lowborn suitor with arsenic in 1857, still be known? For if Madeleine Smith was singled out by society, her character and her story (in its peculiar 'exceptionalness') reflect more on the prejudices and driving mores of the unrecorded faces that watched her during her trial than on herself. The past slips in so gradually – the long shot of Glasgow is not that conspicuously modern to begin with; the blare of auto horns over the shot only vaguely suggests anything beyond 1910; the footsteps on the track might just as well be Emile L'Angelier's – that the final question mark will punctuate not merely a query of guilt or innocence, but whose guilt? and when?

That ending is also a part of Lean's synthesis of Victorian art and letters that began with Dickens. For like the variant endings of *Great Expectations,* the issue of Madeleine's guilt is genuinely uncertain. Moreover, it can remain central only as long as it is unresolved. *Madeliene* is neither fact nor fable. It refuses to do more than speculate on what really happened not because of historical accuracy (the trial jury recorded a non-committal verdict of 'Not proven') but because it is appropriate to the historical ambivalence that confronted the real Madeleine Smith, because a large part of this personal history's impact derives from changing values, from the reasons why Madeleine's letters which now seem so full of girlish frivolity and almost cloyingly genteel in their ardor (how else can one explain the lingering chastity of the affair and the hundreds of guilty words exchanged trying to justify the 'sin' that finally overcame it; 'Am I not your wife? Yes I am. And you may rest assured that after what has passed I cannot be the wife of any other but dear, dear Emile [though] we should, I suppose, have waited till we were married.' *May 6, 1856)* were labelled scandalous, torrid, or 'frightful' (the term used by John Inglis, Madeleine's defense attorney) at the time. Ultimately the only answer one could honorably make to the accusing finger of Victorian society (the one Madeleine tries unsuccessfully to make to its most prominent representative, her father) was no answer.

*   *   *   *   *

In a sense, *Madeleine* is original material (not based on a Coward play or Dickens novel).* As with many of his earlier films the character herself and 'her strange Romantic story' fall strikingly, with a minumum of manipulation, into line with Lean's pre-conceptions. Because of films like *Bridge On The River Kwai, Lawrence,* or the Dickens adaptations, it would be difficult to defend a contention that Lean is a distinct feminist. But beginning with *Brief Encounter* and culminating with *Ryan's Daughter,* Lean has constructed several of his films around a heroine. Madeleine is one; like Laura Jesson and Mary Justin (in *Passionate Friends)* before, she is caught in a stifling trap of social conventions – a trap that was much more rigidly built in 1857 – and brought very near to destruction. But even more than Laura or Mary, even more than Jane Hudson in *Summer Madness* or Rosy Ryan, Madeleine is, as the title suggests, the entire film. Perhaps it is not from as subjective a viewpoint as Pip or Laura Jesson (although several images do emerge directly from her inner state); but since the very indeterminateness of her motives, her 'secret,' are the focal point of her trial – in both a legalistic and moral sense – that approach to her emotions would not necessarily be apt. More importantly, whatever the real Madeleine Smith was, however sordid or everyday, whatever the authentic Emile, or William Minnoch, or Glasgow of 1857, Lean displaces them all to concentrate on a lustrous Romantic portrait of an enigmatic young girl, and a woman who in the final analysis may be the unhappiest of his heroines.

---

* Although she has also been the subject of at least two novels, the first published in 1864, and a tragi-comedy in two acts (1928).

Madeleine's personal fantasies and the deterministic undercurrent first detected in the quasi-objectivity of the prologue (with its dry, narrative voice-over) are set up rapidly and economically. From the modern street a period figure emerges and casts her compelling shadow over a 'for sale' sign; Madeleine (Ann Todd) appears and smiles vaguely. 'Madeleine. . . come, my dear, we're going in,' her mother calls; inside the house the camera and the Smith family glide fatefully towards each other. Mr. Smith, the architect, the cold pragmatist, is impressed ('It has solidity'); Madeleine is fascinated. A pan strays with her as she drifts to the stairwell and descends to the basement rooms – there she fixes on a barred window and a tracking shot follows her over. As light from it strikes the wall behind her, a shadow falls across her face and is greeted by another smile. Quickly the muted symbols of the room are suggested: the predestined pull of the travelling and panning; the window which draws Madeleine forward like an unseen hand; the anticipation by the shadow and the bars of Emile and the prison (both in the way he is first seen and in the figurative sense of a 'shadow over her existence'); •the furtiveness of a 'lower' room; the sexuality of its womb-like security and the narrow opening which Emile will violate with his cane. But her look – transfigured as violins swell over shot, a lyrical solo followed by anticipatory tremuloes – and all that she 'sees' can never be fully probed. How well she knows Emile, whether she knows him at all, at this point, is never specified (although her mother's remark later, 'Madeleine, I've never heard you sing in French before,' intimates that her acquaintance is not too long standing). Uncertainty is a factor from the beginning. For L'Angelier will arrive as if created to fit the opportunity, as if conceived and conjured up by Madeleine as she enters that dark chamber. And with that darkness clinging to him, a dream-lover or a demon-lover or both, he is sprung from the depths of house and soul to fulfil her Romantic yearnings.

That aspect, at least, is clear from the start. Madeleine's romantic fancies are reflected in her ending to Janet's bedtime story ('You haven't finished telling me what happened to the Prince?' 'He went far away across the sea. . . and never came back again.') with even a presentiment of tragedy. Immediately after, while she sings a French ballad in the parlor, *her* 'foreign prince' arrives outside. At first, he is only a long, black shadow across the pavement, then a pair of glistening boots as a medium close shot slowly pans up the length of his body. The real Pierre Emile L'Angelier was the son of an immigrant French nurseryman; he worked as an unimportant clerk in a warehouse. The film L'Angelier also holds this position. He too takes drugs (laudanum) for energy, lives in a modest flat in Franklin Place, and even seems a trifle pathetic in his struggle against his own foppish outlays for financial security. But when he stands outside Madeleine's basement window at night, he bears only a superficial resemblance to those L'Angeliers. His eyes are inflamed in a dusky face, and a pleased, almost smug smile disturbs the line of his pencil moustache. Swathed in a velvet cape and twirling a silver-topped cane, he looms up suddenly, brooding and awesome in stature, a consummate Byronic figure in full regalia. Madeleine is trapped inside for a moment, confined in a long medium shot as the family and her formal suitor, William Minnoch, make their ritual goodnights. Then, like a good stage director, she brings down the lights. A cut to high angle causes her figure to be distorted by the lamp glass in the foreground as she moves about the room (foreshadowing a latter distortion by an apothecary jar at the druggists); a rapturous waltz surges on the track; a low angle medium close shot catches the edge of her dress swirling excitedly past. Four cane taps, a key is passed – on the landing without, Emile is waiting. They stand together silhouetted against the street light, their faces intercut in deeply backlit close-ups, obscure, barely discernible features with highlights on the eyes and lips, a stylized vision. They kiss and ignite a real storm, a torrent of passion that threatens to drench them as thoroughly as any physical love would.

Much of the magnetism of L'Angelier's character is rendered figuratively or in archetype. Superficially he is something of a *poseur;* metaphysically, storms seem to accompany his passage. In the first actual lovemaking, Madeleine meets him on the grounds of the country house at Rowaleyn. There on an idyllic, sheltered hilltop, overlooking the moonlit sea, they listen to the raucous strains of a distant dance. Impulsively, she invites Emile to join her in a highland reel ('Dance with me. We are quite alone.' 'I do not know how.' 'Danse avec moi.') At first, he will do no more than prance satyr-like and tap his palm with his cane; she weaves slowly around him. Lean cuts to the dancers in the village then back as an impatient Madeleine snatches away his symbolic stick ('It should go faster . . You can't dance with that in in your hand.') Another cut: a travelling shot with those below as they pick up speed. In the woods, Madeleine falls. In close shot Emile's self-assured smile re-asserts itself, and he bends towards her. The sequence ends on the others, in various cuts, spinning, gyrating, shouting, until one feverish couple can dance no more, turn, and run out.

But this is nearer the end than the beginning of the affair. On a narrative level, the change in Madeleine's attitude is pin-pointed when she visits L'Angelier's rooms:

> MADELEINE:
> Take me away, Emile, Take me away
> before it is too late.
>
> EMILE:
> Where?
>
> MADELEINE:
> Well, you have work offered you in
> London. We could be happy there.
>
> EMILE: (sarcastically)
> Happy. Do you think we can be happy
> on what I earn?
>
> MADELEINE:
> If you love me, yes.

EMILE:

No, this is not what I desire. If we
marry, we marry into your life, not mine.
You will keep your word and speak to your
father. . . .

MADELEINE: (emphatically)

Will you marry me, Emile?

EMILE:

Under such circumstances, no. (A long
pause) What are you doing?

MADELEINE:

Emile, I wonder if you know what you have
done to me. I . . . I thought we loved each
other. I wanted to leave my family and go
away with you. But, until now, I have never
really known you.

EMILE:

Nothing has changed.

MADELEINE:

It has, Emile.

Why it has changed only becomes apparent in the shifting imagery that
characterises L'Angelier's scenes, in his diminishing stature in Madeleine's
eyes. For on this level, Madeleine's real disillusionment comes later.
Throughout the first two thirds of the picture (the events before the
trial), Lean will use certain motifs and interior moods to expand the
implications of his scenes. As Madeleine's disenchantment grows, L'Angelier degenerates from Byronic hero to an affected, intemperate dandy.
Part of his appeal had always been simply his foreignness and his good
looks, and the very forbiddenness of the affair. That was evident from the
first scene in the parlor: 'Dis moi tu m'aime,' Madeleine sang, obviously

enjoying the thrill of addressing her lover in the very midst of her unknowing family, and at the same time vaguely aware of the immaturity of her conduct ('I was clumsy; I sang many wrong notes.'). Her breathless observation to Emile ('We are like children hiding. . .') and her later invitation to dance were simply exhortations to play the 'illicit' game with her. Nor is L'Angelier completely immune (his neighbor, Thuau, calls Madeleine an 'enchantress' and quotes Emile's remark, 'It is a perfect fascination I have for that girl,' at the trial). Yet he clings to the notion of marrying only into Madeleine's life and caste of society (his smug remark about his new necktie, 'I chose it with care,' might easily apply to Madeleine herself). Much of this is fraught with irony. 'There is such a thing as keeping up appearances,' he tells Thuau, defending the purchase of an expensive suit. 'There is such a thing as paying the rent, too,' his friend replies, not realizing that for L'Angelier the one depends on the other. To 'protect his investment' and maintain his hold on Madeleine, L'Angelier must, literally and figuratively, make his presence felt – a necessity which Lean underscores. When, for example, Madeleine accepts Minnoch at the ball, he opens his mouth to answer her, but a wail of bagpipes drowns him out. Shortly thereafter, a cut to a high angle view of the ballroom discloses L'Angelier's figure on a balcony in the foreground of the shot. A reverse frames him, sullen and almost Satanic, closely and at a low angle. The music is associated with the tryst at Rowaleyn, and the manner of its intrusion here while L'Angelier lurks ubiquitously (he seems from his position to hold sway over the entire room and its occupants) suggests that Minnoch *is* 'drowned out' and might still be easily displaced by the former lover (and will be, but more by the effects of his ceasing to be present than anything else).

L'Angelier's threat to blackmail Madeleine into wedlock ('You made yourself my wife.') becomes understandable to those with ironic insight into his all-too-human failings. But for Madeleine it is Don Juan cast into a dismal flat exuding vulgar insecurity. The highly dramatic rendering of the sequence in which L'Angelier forces his way into the house – her childish amusement in gazing at her new hat in the mirror yielding to a

Madeleine

Emile L'Angelier (Ivan Desny) seethes with jealousy as he watches Madeleine (Ann Todd) dance happily with Mr Minnoch (Norman Woland).

Above: Emile L'Angelier (Ivan Desny) refuses to elope with Madeleine (Ann Todd).

Left: Thuau (Eugene Deckers) tells Mr Smith (Leslie Banks) that his daughter Madeleine (Ann Todd) had been intimate with the recently murdered L'Angelier (Ivan Desnay).

tracking shot which is suddenly interrupted; the ominous rasp of the cane behind the closed curtain; the equally ominous geometry of an abrupt tilt from the taut door chain to a face wedged in the narrow vertical opening by the jamb; low light moving hesitantly with Madeleine down the corridor; the panning medium close shot across her prostrate, sobbing form – all fittingly mark the end of a 'Romance,' of which Madeleine is author as much as participant, the brutish transformation of Lochinvar into Caliban.

The final irony is that more than anything vanity works against L'Angelier, perhaps doubly against him (if Madeleine is guilty) in the cosmetic purposes for which she originally purchases the arsenic as well as in his own posturing. Aware of this, Lean adds numerous sardonic touches to the scene with the cocoa. Some are extremely apparent, such as the sound montage of the doorbell (rung by L'Angelier) over an extra close shot of the bottle of poison. The constant favoring of the fateful cup in the framing may be a bit forced when it is the subject of a follow focus from the close foreground as Madeleine says 'Take this to Monsieur' over shot; but it has a tensely ambiguous effect later, in a high angle medium close shot of her, when it hovers hazily at the bottom of the frame. Some are fairly subtle: Emile's casual 'I fear that . . . ' interrupted by the maid's entry with the tray of chocolate and empty cups. Others are complex visual and aural metaphors, as when Madeleine pours some of the arsenic into a wash basin while Janet bathes in the background and sings, 'Who killed Cock Robin.' The inference is not just of murder in general. By this point it is clear that it refers more specifically to L'Angelier, the cockerel with fancy tie displayed like a coxcomb. Moments later Emile enters with exaggerated sound effects: the clack of his walking stick into the stand, the thump of his gloves into his hat – he struts through the parlor, preening in front of the mirror, condescendingly appreciating the furnishings, and boasting just a little ('I have inherited the feelings and delicacies of a person well bred. . .'). But, as he leans against the mantlepiece, his real stature and, irrevocably, his death are reflected behind him in the form of a small statuette: a brass rooster. The metamorphosis is complete. The symbolic reduction of Emile from an almost preternatural level to an animal one defines the change in him which Madeleine had sensed somewhat inexactly before.

There are two principle consequences. The first – Emile's death – occurs within the context of Lean's pantheistic forces. A brief shot catches the wind sweeping a cobbled street. Again L'Angelier's shadow stretches over it (but this time he wears a light colored coat, as if the loss of aura forbade anything as dark as in his first appearance). Again it starts to rain. The next sequence begins with an establishing shot of a clock face reading 11.25. Lean condenses the passage of ninety-five minutes into a half dozen deterministic cuts: L'Angelier outside pondering the unlit windows of the house; Madeleine and Janet asleep within. Then, as if the course of things were truly beyond human intervention come four shots that are purely 'objective:' a corridor filled with creaking noises; the front door straining against the gusts; the lock, its bolt rattling; and finally a street clock. In a distant tower one a.m. sounds like a knell; it sets in motion a precipitous tilt down which reveals L'Angelier's figure – a walking stick detaches itself and falls to the wet pavement, the form sags.

The second consequence is on a subjective level. For just as L'Angelier's death will be carried, literally, in the wind, Madeleine unconsciously discerns the need to shelter herself from the storms that attend his passing and buffet the house in the night, the need for a safe harbor. That this is her view of Minnoch is clearly established in one of their exchanges:

> MINNOCH:
> Madeleine, will you wear this ring. . .
> till we chose you one. (he shows it to her)
> It will be clumsy on your hand, but I should
> like to think of it there.
>
> MADELEINE:
> I will wear it. I like it. 'Tis
> solid. Is it your crest?

MINNOCH: (nodding)
A crossbow.

MADELEINE:
Ah. I thought it was an
anchor.

Like his ring Minnoch is solid; like Fred Jesson, or Howard Justin, pulling his wife back from the subway tracks, he is the anchor that will keep Madeleine off the shoals of passion. Caught as she is in the opposing currents of social convention and adventurous infatuation, threatened leewardly and windwardly by their respective incarnations in her father and L'Angelier, Minnoch offers the refuge of a relationship free of anxiety. And if he lacks fire, Lean compensates partially by setting his proposals to Madeleine against backgrounds that are 'acceptably' Romantic: riding by the sea and at the ball.

Like her antecedents in Lean's work, Madeleine is poised between domestic security and the frightening abyss of independence. What makes Madeleine unique (beyond her willingness, at one point at least, to abandon all and leave with her lover) is the bi-focal quality of her character, partially deriving from the ill-defined nature of the actual Madeleine Smith, and partially a synthesis of fictional personalities as diverse as Laura Jesson and Estella. The similarity with the former, between Madeleine's idealization of Emile and Laura's fantasy visions of Romantic love through the train window, is clear enough. The links with Estella, the beginnings of unemotional demeanor, are not forged until the last third of the picture. But just as surely as Emile ceases being analogous to the noble Alec Harvey and emerges an arrogant Bentley Drummle, as Minnoch becomes less a weak Fred Jesson and acquires some of Pip's final resolution, Madeleine, to save herself, must become as intangible, mysterious, and coldly inaccessible as Estella. For when the real and imagined L'Angelier both perish, it is no longer possible to hide from the fury of righteous winds.

Up until that point Madeleine had used her father's ignorance of her

98

lover to heighten her own sense of security, to rise above his unfeeling reserve (while psychologically compensating for his lack of affectionate display towards her) and to insulate herself from his gruff authoritarianism. Even in the scene where she knelt at his feet, helping with his boots and listening to his chastisement ('There seems to be something about your character that prevents you from acting naturally'), she remained mentally above him. This position was re-inforced by the sea of crinoline dress spread about her which materially simulates the expansiveness of her inner sensation and allows her to dominate the frame. Through the two-dimensional area which the dress as an extension of self takes up and in the whiteness of it against her father's black and grey in the dimly lit room, she is made, despite being at his feet, the visual center.

Immediately after L'Angelier's death, a medium shot catches Madeleine in white again (her wedding dress), again unconcernedly trying something on before a mirror and this time made ominously double-headed by the framing. When she confronts Thuau (who has come to expose her) and Mr. Smith in the study, the last two shots disclose a subtle shift of psychological balance. Smith stands in the foreground. The camera adjusts to a slightly higher angle, looking down as she comes up behind him. His line, 'We are naked,' applies principally to Madeleine, stripped of her secrecy. (The decor underlines her assailability, a pale figure all in white surrounded by Smith and Thuau's dark suits and the dark wood paneling and leather chairs.) Again she goes down on her knees before her father, but this time she falls clutching his legs for support. The medium close shot of her as Smith frees himself and leaves the room – his figure in the background now dominates, caught from a low angle – are in marked contrast with the earlier scene. The angle and framing now accentuate the physical vulnerability. With everything out in the open, she can no longer control the situation.

As her superior position deteriorates, Madeleine's ability to resist the encroachments of the real world into her personal universe diminishes. At the railway station, her physical escape from Glasgow is rendered unfeasible by Minnoch. She returns his ring ('It may get lost.') with all its implications. She drifts away from him, out of safe harbor, and loses herself in the crowd, in her own thoughts.

*   *   *   *   *

Various images reappear decisively in the trial, a sequence which occupies the final third of the film. With only her interior resolve and a black veil to shield her, Madeleine enters the coutroom from the cellar prison (a low angle pan up stressing the steepness of the ascent). Analogously, she is being drawn out of her own room in the basement of Blytheswood Square. The sound of the trap door dropping shut startles her, suggests her disorientation at being pulled up forcibly out of her own world. (The exterior shot of the courthouse itself revealed it against the sky cut off from the gray solidity of the city.) Her loss of privacy in the thronging court is emphasized by an insert of faces peering through oval-shaped ports in the doors of the room and a shot of an artist sketching her in stern profile. The clerk reading the indictment, the judge squinting over his spectacles, the murmurs of the officials – all are contiguous to her anxious emergence. As Madeleine has mentally withdrawn into unperturbable silence (almost as casually it seems as she lowered her black veil over her face), Lean divides the trial episode clearly between subjective and objective.

Among the sights and sounds of the proceedings, Madeleine fixes on the ringing of the court bell, the table with her possessions on exhibit, and (as Minnoch is being cross-examined) the black boots of the prosecutor moving across the floor. The details Madeleine picks out – or those Lean selects for her – build a psychological rather than physical reality. Her disinterest in Minnoch on the stand, for example, stems from her realization that she can no longer anchor herself for safety to anyone. But beyond that, Lean is stacking the case in Madeleine's favor.

On a large scale the trial itself is intricately but precisely arranged. The prosecution has but four witnesses on screen; the defense has nine. Moreover the Lord Advocate is 'forced' to present his case in capsule chronology; Inglis develops his out of the framework of his impassioned closing remarks with witnesses in flashback close shots at the appropriate moments. By the time he finally concludes, striding dramatically into a tight close shot, Lean has edited the prosecution out of any chance of victory.

All this might be justified as merely affirming the authentic course of the trial; but it is also the climax to a consistent pattern through which, by using actual events but altering them slightly, Lean manages simultaneously to approach and circumvent historical reality. In the composition of shots (such as the empty medicine glass in the foreground with Madeleine's picture, visually anticipating Inglis' suggestions of possible suicide), in simple narrative selection (for example, the movie Madeleine is seen using the arsenic on her skin, something the real Madeleine Smith claimed but could never prove), in the direction of action (Ann Todd's expression of faint but apparently genuine surprise on hearing that Emile is dead), Lean subliminally prepares the viewer for the trial, for the lengthy speeches delivered by prosecution and defense directly to the camera (equating the jury and the audience) and for the final verdict.

Accordingly, by the second time the trap falls destiny has already dealt in Madeleine's favor. Lean cuts to a long shot: the courtroom is less crowded, not as constricting, the tension dissipated. At the verdict, a tracking shot towards Madeleine in the dock dissolves to a view of her on the steps of the courthouse, parasol in hand, again a portrait of aloof beauty and gentility. Unlike most of Lean's dreamers and visionaries, who are either destroyed by their dream or compelled to abandon it, Madeleine has retained her integrity and isolation. If for no other reason perhaps than in her search for something beyond her assigned lot, she has (like the equally exceptional 'dreamer' Ridgefield, in *The Sound Barrier* forged an internal strength. Her remark to Minnoch – 'I do not regret things' – is prophetic and at the same time characteristic. As the quietly beautiful face and Gioconda smile appear in final medium close shot, the narrator asks, 'Madeleine Smith, ye have heard the indictment. Were ye guilty or not guilty?' She moves her head slightly from side to side, but

101

her eyes remain fixed on the camera as it travels in slowly towards her. There is no answer.

Nor should there be one. Objective recreation has never been one of Lean's aims. Rather, just as the artist who sat sketching Madeleine was not rendering a likeness of Ann Todd, of the reality before him,* but of what he imagined a murderess should resemble, Lean 'interprets' history. Unlike him, Lean does not phenomenologically fit people to real occurrences, but, conversely, molds events to *his* characters. If this film is to remain textured by dreams, 'to venture into [Coleridge's] twilight realms. . . and feel deep interest in modes of inmost being,' those modes cannot be restricted. The vague smile and barely perceptible travelling in of the opening scene return and fade again, the enigma is all that remains.

---

* The artist's sketch *is* a real one, taken from a contemporary newspaper drawing. Since no photographs of Madeleine Smith are extant, it is perhaps, by questioning the reliability of the artist's graphics, a way of suggesting that the legends of her beauty (which justify her being portrayed by Ann Todd rather than a character actress who 'looked' the part) might be true after all. The real sketch also reveals that the black veil is an original concept of the film. But these revelations (and even more fleeting ones, such as the identicalness of the two Madeleines' handwriting evidenced in a very brief insert close shot of a letter addressed to L'Angelier) are obviously not available to the general audience.

Chapter 5

THE SOUND BARRIER (1952)

Thou art a symbol and a sign
To Mortals of their fate and force;
Like thee, Man is in part divine,
A troubled stream from a pure source;
And Man in portions can foresee
His own funereal destiny,
His wretchedness, and his resistance,
And his sad unallied existence;
To which his Spirit may oppose
Itself – and equal to all woes,
And a firm will, and a deep sense,
Which even in torture can descry
Its own concenter'd recompense,
Triumphant where it dares defy,
And making death a Victory.

George Gordon, Lord Byron,
'Prometheus'

IT WOULD BE simple to label *The Sound Barrier* as an entertaining semi-documentary about the men who challenged the speed of sound, to argue

that with *Madeleine* and this new venture Lean's career had taken a turn
back up the 'documentarian' road in the direction of *In Which We Serve*
– easy but inaccurate. In Lean's films, the definition of milieu, whether
the brick and cobblestone of Victorian London or the tinted glass and
concrete of supersonic aviation, is a means not an end; 'appearance' is
only one facet of a more complex reality. It is not surprising that
contemporary critical assessments of *The Sound Barrier* failed to understand what Lean was actually detailing.

Man in flight *is* the central concern of this motion picture. Initially, all
the elements which characterize the detached, understated tradition of the
GPO shorts and the faithful recreations of Jennings seem present. The
scientific and/or technical details of the actual endeavor (such as
Ridgefield's explanation of the 'sound barrier' or his demonstration of jet
propulsion in the factory; the many faithfully recreated test flights) are
included. But the elevation of events over the characters, the definition of
the objective at the expense of the personal are only formally inherent
tendencies. Their application in *The Sound Barrier* is restricted and never
becomes part of a documentary exposition.

The scene of Ridgefield's explanation of the barrier, for example, is
only superficially technical. In the middle of an informal supper with his
daughter, Sue, and son-in-law, Tony, he uses a ruler as a prop and
delivers an impromptu lecture, trying to outline the intangible in simple
terms for the uncomprehending Sue. But as he does, her expression
reveals a lingering uncertainty – not just over the 'how's' of the operation
but over the 'why's' as well. She verbalizes her qualms later that evening:

> SUE:
> Father, answer me a question, will you?
>
> RIDGEFIELD:
> Yes.
>
> SUE:
> Is the ability to travel at two thousand miles an
> hour going to be a blessing to the human race?

RIDGEFIELD:
Well, I'd say that's up to the human race.

SUE:
As a member of it, *I* can't say that I'm duly
optimistic. In fact, if that's all that lies beyond
this barrier, what purpose is there in risking
lives to crash it?

RIDGEFIELD:
Well, I could talk about the national
security . . . beating the potential enemy
bomber . . . flying to New York in two hours.
But that's not the real point. The real point is
it's just got to be done. What purpose did
Scott have in going to the South Pole?

SUE:
I wish I knew. I really wish I knew.

This dialogue describes the basis of the most important personal conflict
in the film – the visionary versus the pragmatist. Ridgefield is alone in
medium close shot when he speaks, figuratively and literally separated
from his daughter. But he is too caught up, too fascinated by the concept
he 'holds in his hand' to take note of his alienation from her and, by
extension, from the world in general.

The scene in the test bed, where Ridgefield gives another demonstration (this time of his new jet engine), functions similarly. Again
Ridgefield, with Tony, is separated from Sue – in the first scene by their
shared knowledge of the sound barrier, in the second by a safety screen
of wire and glass. For although Tony is clearly not driven by any abstract
ideals or sense of 'mission,' his feelings are a reflection of admiration for
those qualities embodied in Ridgefield (his scatter-brained inanities –
singing 'I'd rather have a bow-wow-wow-wow-wow' or irritating his
wife with trite phrases like 'piece of cake' – mark him simply as a boorish

but likeable fellow); and their intensity places him side-by-side with Ridgefield in that chamber and on the brink of the equally perilous realms of the unexplored. During Sue's first jet flight she continually stares down at the earth (the Alps, the Greek ruins) below her, until a newly-inspired Tony tells her, echoing Ridgefield's own words, 'Why do you want to look at the poor old earth? Look up there. There's our future: Space. You can't make that insignificant.' Along with Tony, Will Sparks, the engineer; Philip Peel; and the other test pilots are instruments of the 'old man's' vision but not unconscious ones. Like Icarus in legend, these men revel in the exhilaration of flight. In the unnatural wind from the jet's engines which disturbs the stalks at the edge of the airfield, they have the power to affect nature, even if only temporarily. The white jet trail curving across the sky is their mark emblazoned over the Andromeda Galaxy (which Lean dissolves to), over the universe. In this context, the test flights assume quasi-mythic proportions. The impassioned voices of the aviators and the sun glinting off their dusky face masks as they buffet towards the unknown have more a connotation of religious litany, as they shout the mach numbers, or costumed ritual than scientific experiment. In these vehicles, veering towards the sun, there is a chance for apotheosis. They may disappear into the void but not before a personal, almost existential, assertion of identity. 'And man in portions can foresee/His own funereal destiny . . . To which his spirit may oppose.'

It is Ridgefield, watching the flights from the ground, who has the acute awareness of 'destiny,' who fulfills the archetypal imagery:

> TONY:
> Oh, by the way, Will wants a name for her
> [the new jet]. Got any ideas, Dad?
>
> RIDGEFIELD:
> Yes. 'Prometheus.'
>
> TONY:
> Prometheus? Who was He?

106

SUE:
He was a Greek god.

RIDGEFIELD:
He stole fire from heaven.

TONY:
Oh, yes, I remember. He came to a sticky end,
didn't he?

RIDGEFIELD:
He did. But the world got fire.

Ridgefield is the 'modern Prometheus.' Instead of stealing fire, his fate is
to break through the gods' mysterious wall of sound. As a pilot, he had
once experienced the elation of flight with metal wings. Now, in his later
years, he has taken to the world of 'imagination.'* He designs the kind
of vehicles which will someday trace a course to the very stars he studies
so fervently in his observatory. He has, in fact, withdrawn so far into his
own world that he seems to lack all human emotions. His 'way of feeling
grief' after his son's fiery death is to examine a model of his new jet and,
after Tony's annihilation, to listen to the tapes of the crash. His vision is
his one, insular passion. As Will Sparks remarks to him, 'I don't know
what devil it is that's eating you up, but it can't make life any too happy
for you.' Ridgefield foreshadows T. E. Lawrence in deed and word: 'The
dreamers of the day are dangerous men.' Frequently lost in thought or
distracted, Ridgefield *is* a 'day dreamer.' Like Lawrence, he consciously
denies the human side of his character and purposely separates himself
from normal society. Alone in his observatory he can watch 'the process
of continuous creation' without danger; outside of it, the threat of
extinction is needed to sustain and compel his actions.

The crisis in Ridgefield's life, like that in Lawrence's, comes when his
humanity re-asserts itself.

---

* Imagination in the sense Coleridge described 'as a repetition in the finite mind of the eternal
act of creation in the infinite I AM.'

The Sound Barrier

Top: Ridgefield (Ralph Richardson) listens to the radio exchanges between the test pilot and ground control from his office in this scene from *The Sound Barrier.*

Bottom: Will Sparks (Joseph Tomelty) and Ridgefield (Ralph Richardson) view films of Tony's crash.

Left: Susan (Ann Todd) and Tony (Nigel Patrick) read of the death of a test pilot of a rival aircraft company.

Below: Will Sparks (Joseph Tomelty), Ridgefield's engineer, counsels his employer to give up his experiments before it cost more lives.

SUE:
You want me to think of you as a man with a
vision. Well, that vision has killed both my
husband and my brother. And while I'm alive
it's not going to kill my son, too. There are
evil visions as well as good ones, you know,
father . . .

[Ridgefield answers while waiting fearfully for
Philip Peel's attempt to break through the barrier.]

RIDGEFIELD: (shaken)
Can a vision be evil, Sue? Can it, can it? It's a
terrible thing to make a man doubt everything
he's ever lived for . . as if I've killed them both
for nothing. But it can't be true. Can it? Can
it?

As Peel's plane dives, the camera, in close on the terrified Ridgefield, tilts
(as it did for Laura Jesson, to subjectify a moment of emotional ins-
tability). But this time the test succeeds; the barrier is broken. In the final
scene, Ridgefield has again withdrawn into his observatory, his doubts
buried. He survives the psychological buffeting of uncertainty because his
visionary shield, his mental conditioning is strong enough.

So central is that vision, good or evil, to *The Sound Barrier* that all the
secondary characters are defined in terms of their relationship to it. Of
those who perish, Chris, Ridgefield's only son, on whom he initially
builds his hopes (forcing him to become a flier), functions primarily as
a symbol of Ridgefield's inability to regenerate his vision, to pass on its
adventurous spirit. Chris' fear of flight (his many lessons prove useless)
and his cowering before his tyrannical father – the force of whose
presence is captured even before he appears by the imposing portrait in
his study – give evidence that he has inherited the very character weak-
nesses which Ridgefield has suppressed in himself. In that sense,

Ridgefield's mute acceptance of Chris' crash during his first solo becomes another tacit assertion of his own uniqueness.

Tony replaces Chris as Ridgefield's protege and student. Immediately after the funeral, Ridgefield uses the glistening model to draw Tony away from Sue, to enmesh him. Framed with Ridgefield in two-shot by the window or leaving his wife's bed to gaze out from the terrace into the black abyss (accompanied by atonal musical strains – suggesting, in Lean's work, fear and wonder), he is the Icarus who flies too near the sun and is thrown back to earth (his ship, upon impact, is buried in the ground).

Of those who survive, Philip Peel, the war pilot who tries to quit flying, is probably the most balanced character. Although his return to aviation is partially in response to an addictive impulse (as he watches Tony and Sue leave Egypt in a jet transport, the music soars and the camera moves into his eager, anticipatory expression), it is not treated as a regression. It is rather a step forward, out of the Egyptian kind of antiquity which Tony had rejected earlier. Mentally, Peel is keener than Tony. He respects Ridgefield's vision and, unlike Tony who is hard put to explain his father-in-law, can detachedly express his admiration (as he says to Sue, 'You know I don't think that sort of understanding comes from up here [pointing to his head] . . . only from here [pointing to his heart]'). But Peel has not subdued his common human feelings. He remains devoted to his family and provides a refuge for Sue after her husband's death. His admirable ability to walk the fine line between the two worlds is best exemplified in the scene following his 'historic'' flight. he returns to his locker room and tries to tell his wife what he has just accomplished:

> JESS: (entering)
> Oh, good. I found you.
>
> PHILIP:
> Hello, darling . . . I . . . I

JESS:
Hello, darling . . . I want to see
you today . . .

      [their dialogue overlaps]
They won't take it back until closing time
tonight.

      [showing him some material]
So we've got to make up our minds now. Do
you think the color's too much?

      [Philip is unable to get a word in]
Because they've got one, sort of a daisy color
with stripes going down here . . . I . . . well, it
seemed a bit dull to me, but if you . . . Look,
darling, pay attention. This is very important.
It is all right?

PHILIP:
Yes, I'm sorry, darling. Yes, it's fine. Come
and see the . . .

JESS: (cutting him off)
Good, that's lovely . . . If I can only get back in
time. Well, 'bye.
'Bye, all. See you at home.

[She leaves. Philip begins to laugh then breaks
down completely]

Though he has tasted briefly of the 'part divine,' Peel must now readjust
to the ordinary. He alone among the protagonists possesses the
equanimity to both crash through the barrier and to confront the mundane aspects of life with a similar (if unequal) enthusiasm.

    Sue, finally, is the vision's antagonist. She neither understands nor
meekly condones the venture. Because her life is built upon home and a
man, her worries those of everyday life, the sound barrier has no meaning

in her 'scheme' of things. To her it is only a 'great wall in the sky strong enough to smash an aircraft to pices . . . beyond it nothing, nothing at all' and her father, cruel and unfeeling. Only after witnessing his human and comprehensible fear of failure during Peel's test run can she even consider a reconciliation. She brings her son with her to Ridgefield's home and sets the child (christened John after his grandfather) on a map of the moon – presaging, possibly, his astronautical future. The final image – Ridgefield's telescope and a model aircraft nosed towards the distant stars – recapitulates within a single frame the central thrust of the film: Ridgefield, the Promethean man, and his legacy of questing for the infinite.

Chapter 6

HOBSON'S CHOICE (1954)

> The brain may devise laws for the
> blood, but a hot temper leaps o'er
> a cold decree. . . – this reasoning
> is not in the fashion to choose me
> a husband.
>
> *The Merchant of Venice*

HOBSON'S CHOICE, made in 1954, is Lean's last film in black-and-white (and, in light of his avowed preference for color and widescreen, is likely to remain so). It also marks his final effort to date set in mid-Victorian Great Britain, the concluding installment in an informal series begun with *Great Expectations.*

The opening of *Hobson's Choice* is closer to the startling, expressionistic prologue of *Oliver Twist* than the documentary-like introduction of *Madeleine.* The wind sweeps loudly down a wet, cobbled street at night. A black boot hangs forebodingly at the top of the frame, as the camera travels back past a trade sign swaying noisily on its rusty hinges to the flickering front lamp of Henry Hobson's shoe store. A cut inside and the

115

travelling continues down a display of Hobson's wares before panning abruptly to a branch tapping against a skylight in the rear. As the camera turns back towards the center of the room, the door suddenly bursts open. A shadow looms across the floor, and in the doorway a dark figure lurches like a drunken ghost, until a loud belch on the soundtrack reveals that it is just a plain drunk. Only then does it become apparent that *Hobson's Choice* is a comedy.

Lean's use of the given elements and fixtures of a period for dramatic effect was never fuller than in *Madeleine*. In *Hobson's Choice,* the comic anagram of this becomes a parody of genre style, in particular his own. The atmosphere of the opening is built on ominously exaggerated details (the streets *must* be wet, the wind *must* be blowing, a branch *must* be striking the skylight with its twisted silhouette) and precipitates a greater comic deflation when a character staggers in and turns out to have been neither shot nor stabbed nor plagued by any demon other than rum.

A similar reversal is applied in the scenes of courtship between Maggie Hobson and Will Mossop. Their Sunday meeting starts out as vaguely reminiscent of Alec and Laura's boating excursion in *Brief Encounter.* An extra long shot of them strolling through the green parkways laid out in a complex geometrical pattern dissolves to a medium shot by a riverbank. But the River Irwell is nothing like the pleasant stream in the earlier film. An iron fence, almost capsizing, fronts a single, paint-flecked bench by a stunted flower bed. The clouds in the background are of smoke sent up by the factory chimneys of Salford. In this less than idyllic spot the couple sit and talk; but Lean photographs them in a long take from behind, at a slight high angle, so that the river remains prominently visible for a considerable time. Near them bits of debris drift through its oily surface; beyond a frothy layer of detergent residue floats, almost motionless except for the occasional clusters of bubbles that detach themselves and arise, with perverse romanticism, skyward. Lean is not above satirizing his own images of love and nature (and in this scene, at least, has even anticipated an ecological relevance). Not even the first kiss is sacred. Alec and Laura's took place spontaneously in a dark passageway amid the noise of rushing engines. Maggie must command hers ('Right here in the street?' 'Come on, lad, get it over.'), retreating into a dingy causeway where the only sound on the track is the shallow gurgling on a small sewer that divides the alley behind the couple.

Rather than Rachmaninoff (who might in this instance be, as Madame Arcati suggests, 'too florid'), *Hobson's Choice* is reinforced with a subtly humorous score (by Malcolm Arnold). It makes its presence felt in the initial tracking shots over the rows of pumps and clogs. Calliope-like notes sound a restrained, waltzing air over the ladies' high-top shoes, a more boisterous clip-clopping for the riding boots, and a music box chiming when the children's footwear appears. A few moments later, as Hobson 'falls' upstairs, a precipitous drumroll accompanies the action. Much of the music and effects – from the comic clarinet when he gets up the next morning to a squeaking medicine cabinet near the end echoing the trombone's lament of the main theme – are geared to Hobson, most effectively perhaps in the strange, vibrato orchestration when he chases the moon in a puddle but appropriately throughout.

For *Hobson's Choice* is a character comedy. And the title role, as portrayed by Charles Laughton, is distinctly in the Dickens tradition. The red-nosed tradesman spending too much time at the local tavern (in this case, the aptly named Moonrakers) is a familiar type. With his round, slightly besotted face and a double chin under a flat-topped hat, his large belly protruding behind an extremely wide belt with a huge, glistening buckle, and his thumbs cocked confidently behind the armholes of his waistcoat, Hobson is mostly bluster. He rants against lawyers ('It's a lawyer's job to squeeze a man and squeeze him where his squirming's seen most.'), women ('Female perversity comes from leading an indoor life. Women think they're important because they're washing kitchens.'), and teetotaling ('Life's got to be worth living before I'll live it.') with equal vigor. Yet his shouts of 'I'm master here!' in his own household are easily circumvented, as in this exchange:

MAGGIE:
Dinner's at one o'clock, remember.

117

HOBSON:

Now, look here, Maggie, I set the
hours in this house. It's at one
o'clock because I say it is, not
because you do.

MAGGIE: (wearily)

Yes, father.

HOBSON:

So long as that's clear, I'll go.
 [He exits.]

MAGGIE:

Dinner's at half past. That'll
give him half an hour.

It is soon obvious that Hobson's eldest daughter, Maggie, runs both
house and shop behind her father's back. She is the primmest and most
efficient, the best at avoiding 'muddles' and least likely to incur Hobson's
disapproval by affecting a 'waggin' hump' (a bustle). She is also the cause
of much of his exasperation by being uppish and by refusing to give any
approbation to his drinking. Maggie's lack of servility (she describes
herself as 'strong and proud') is in marked contrast to the sight of her
father on his knees before Mrs. Hepworth, a wealthy patron (who is
prompted to remark, 'Get up, Hobson, you look ridiculous,' which taken
with his middle daughter's urging in the previous scene that he leave the
room so that it might be straightened up furthers the implication that he
has become out of place in his own store) and his hypocritical sort of
pride. Yet for all her cold pragmatism ('Courting's like that, my lass,' she
tells her sister while tapping a sequined shoe, 'all glitter and no use to
anybody.'), she harbors certain Romantic urges, which, like the rose from
her bridal bouquet that she saves from the trash to press in her Bible, are
quietly concealed.

Maggie is the least sentimental, most aggressive of Lean's heroines; so
aggressive, in fact, that she could probably never exist in his work except

118

in a comedy. Like that of the married Laura Jesson or the spinsterish Jane Hudson in *Summer Madness,* her lot seems somehow pre-ordained, as when Hobson announces his intentions for his younger offspring:

> MAGGIE:
> If you're dealing husbands round,
> don't I get one?
>
> HOBSON: (surprised)
> You, with a husband? (laughing
> uncontrollably) Aye, that's a
> good one.
>
> MAGGIE: (coldly)
> Why not?
>
> HOBSON:
> Why not? (pacing about) Now,
> Maggie, I thought you'd sense
> enough to know. Well, if you
> want brutal truth, you're past
> marrying age.
>
> MAGGIE:
> I'm thirty.
>
> HOBSON:
> Aye. Thirty and shelved. Well,
> all the women can't have husbands,
> Maggie

But within Maggie's utilitarian principles is the firm belief that a husband would serve. Accordingly, while another Lean heroine might do no more than wait restlessly for something to happen, Maggie attacks the question frontally ('It's a poor sort of woman that will stay lazy when she sees her best chance slipping from her.'). She announces her own intention to an awed Will Mossop, dismisses his former fiancée ('You're treading on my

119

Hobson's Choice

Dr. McFarlane (John Laurie) examines Hobson (Charles Laughton) after an attack of delirium tremens in this scene from *Hobson's Choice*.

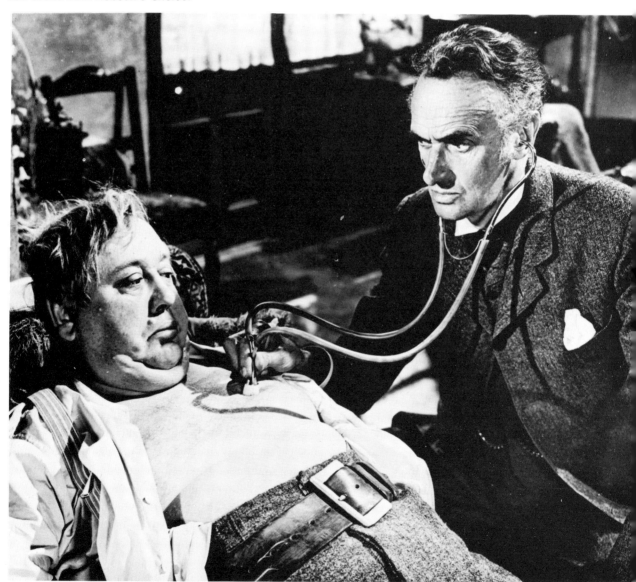

Above: Maggie (Brenda de Banzie) orders a kiss from 'her man' Willie (John Mills).

Below: Hobson (Charles Laughton) in the middle of the dt's.

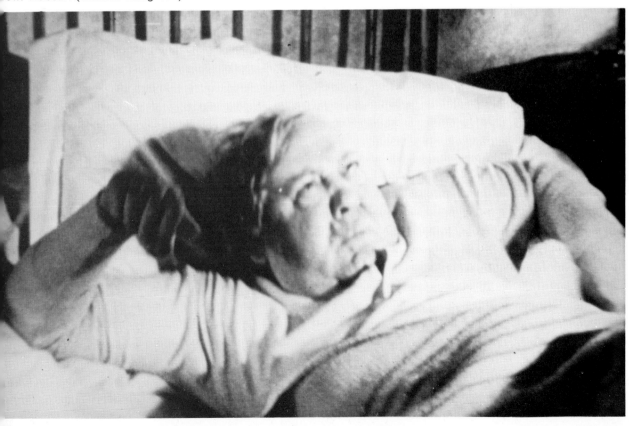

foot.'), picks up a ring (Alice: 'A brass ring? Out of stock?' Maggie: 'Why not. It's always from someone's stock.'), and summons a wedding party to the church. While it may not occur quite as rapidly as all that, it does come about by a wilful design, a design which simultaneously affirms and contradicts her father's sarcastic observation: 'It's a great relief to know your mind's taken up with ideas; I thought for a moment it was taken up with a real man.'

In one sense, Maggie's mind *is* only taken up with an idea. When she says, 'Will Mossop, you're my man,' it may have less to do with Will himself than with the abstract notion of using him to find her own independence. But she, unlike the less fortunate Madeleine, realizes it must be sought in a way the established social order approves of, or rather – as Victorian society did not approve of independent women at all – in a way that was not overtly anti-establishmentarian. In this instance it is through marriage. But Will's confusion reflects the on-going ambivalence of Maggie's having to break several minor traditions (waiting for some man to propose; marrying within her class) in order to fulfil this more basic one (getting a 'man') which, in turn, is only a means towards the end of personal enfranchisement. Maggie views Will as an implement for fashioning her own destiny. As she tells him, 'You're a business idea in the shape of a man. My brains and your hands'll make a working partnership.' In another sense, however, the speech she makes to Mrs. Hepworth to secure a loan betrays a confidence in something more than a tool and a sympathy for someone whom she feels capable of respecting. This is evident from Will's first appearance, when he pops up through the cellar trap and squints at the world like a myopic mole. Maggie makes an excuse for his inability to read a calling card ('It's the italics.') while the editing establishes that she is the only one who can see that he is holding it upside down. But her consideration here and the relationship she subsequently finds with Will involve more than her protecting him or teaching him how to write with the aid of inspirational maxims ('Great things grow from small,' 'There is always room at the top.'). By a kind of transference, she projects her own drives (those socially unacceptable in a female) onto him and succeeds in altering both his outward appearance and his personality. He becomes genuinely 'her man' not just in terms of possession but because she, quite literally, 'makes him.'

In the early stages, Lean clarifies Will's pliability through a variety of comic scenes. The outings in the park is followed by a trip to Will's lodgings. There while Maggie disentangles him from his fiancee and her mother (his landlady), a temperance parade passes advising him to 'Beware the Wrath to Come.' But he is already too caught up in the various possibilities which Maggie has opened up and loses himself in reverie until a blow from his would-be mother-in-law jars him awake. It is too late for him to be wary – Maggie has intoxicated him with dreams of advancement. Gradually, as Will – much like Madeleine was – is figuratively pulled up from the security of his cellar, changes take place. Hobson's attempted intimidation with his black belt ('You've got an ailment and I've got the cure. We'll beat the love from your body.') only succeeds in dispelling his remaining hesitancy. (He evens puns in reply: 'You'll not beat loving me.') From a shot of Willie fidgeting and embarrassed as he watches Maggie test the springs of a double bed, Lean dissolves to him self-assuredly examining sheets of leather. His physical aspect is transformed; the dark circles disappear from under his eyes, the brows become less bushy, his bowl haircut fills out below the ears, and his suits begin to fit. Even his voice mellows (and no longer cracks when threatened, as it did when Hobson called him up for chastisement). There are fuller, maturing implications in his dialogue with Maggie:

> WILL:
> I'm going to give you a shock.
>
> MAGGIE:
> I doubt it.
>
> WILL:
> I've just paid out 120 pounds.
>
> MAGGIE: (shocked)
> What?

WILL:
To Mrs. Hepworth. That's her
capital plus twenty per cent.
We can do without her now.

MAGGIE:
It looks as though you can do
without me, too.

WILL:
Maggie! I thought to please you.

MAGGIE:
You do. You do. Only I like to
have a finger in the pie.

WILL:
God knows, Maggie, you made the
whole pie.

As Will's awareness expands, he moves from his earlier ecstatic visions ('It's like a happy dream.') to a calmer, more stable confidence in the situation. His ultimate realizations are confided to Maggie after he confronts Hobson on equal terms ('You told me to be strong and use the power that's come to me through you. Words came to me mouth that made me jump at me own boldness . . . I said such things . . . to him, while he's the old master.' Maggie: 'And you're the new.'), but the joy of them, like his persistent 'By gum's,' remains his own. The dreams return, this time in concrete and attainable form, because, as Maggie observes (in vicarious triumph), 'You're the man I made you. And I'm proud.'

Throughout *Hobson's Choice* the framing serves to underscore the relationships. From the direct and economic establishment of the setting and period with travelling shots down Chapell Street, Lean elects to insert an over-the-shoulder of Beenstock Senior peering down sternly at the pub and Hobson ('There's a small spark of decency in that man that's telling

124

him, at this very moment, that my eye is on him.'). Inside Moonrakers, an insouciant Hobson is framed tightly by his staunch drinking cronies; but during a later visit when Maggie's conduct makes him the object of some ridicule he will be isolated in medium close shots. In both instances, the framing reflects the attitude of those around Hobson.

On a more complex level, Hobson's own domineering attitude is marked in a scene where Vicky helps him with his boots. As in *Madeleine*, the staging (she is at his feet), angle (over shoulder: up towards him and down at her), and costuming (she is in black; he is white-shirted) favor the dominant character (but this time without the daughter-over-father, against-appearances thrust of the similar sequence in the earlier picture). In many ways, Maggie's defiance is bolder than Madeleine's; and her father's failure to bring her into line is visualized in a four-shot of the family at supper that evening. While he tyrannizes his younger daughters, Hobson stations himself in the foreground taking up a large portion of the frame with his head and shoulders. They stand meekly beyond him to the right; then Maggie enters. As she comes forward unhesitatingly, the visual focus re-aligns itself on her form moving through the shot. When she announces, 'I'm going to marry Will, Father,' she literally turns Hobson's head around, forcibly breaking his overbearing gaze by brushing past him. After the others have been sent out so that they may talk, Lean uses a slight low angle, he sits and she stands determinedly over him ('I've to settle my life's course. . . *I'll* tell you *my* terms.').

The dynamic shift away from Hobson, initiated here, culminates in the final confrontation between the three principals. Lean begins by inter-cutting a slight high angle medium shot of Hobson and all three daughters with a slight low angle of Will in medium close. All are arrayed against his lone figure – his tactic is to imitate Hobson's own swaggering manner. With a haughty tone and his thumbs wedged under his vest, he copies the old master's habitual poses. Hobson, perhaps sensing his ploy, waits until only Will and Maggie remain in the room with him before offering her husband a seat. Then he stands hovering

125

over his daughter and son-in-law, tucks in his thumbs, and tries to gesticulate his way back into control of the scene while making his 'generous proposal.' But Willie rises, backs him down into a chair with a few hard, economic facts ('And all you think you can offer me is me old job at eighteen shillings a week, me, the owner of a business that's starving yours to death.'), and wins the game of dominance and submission handily. When the question of a name for the shop is settled, a panning medium close shot carries Maggie, gazing admiringly, from the loser's (Hobson's) side to Will's.

The presence of three main characters, all significantly interacting, necessarily prevents Lean from subjectifying much of the material by restricting it to any one viewpoint. Nevertheless, there are several instances where a first person attitude is momentarily adopted, generally for comic effect. Willie's reverie outside his old lodgings, for example, is subjectively intensified by a travelling in to close shot and a crescendo on the track. The jolt of being brought out of it is approximated for the audience by cutting back with the sound of the landlady's blow and abruptly replacing the music with street sounds and raucous shouts. A smaller, similar touch is added when Will leaves the new shop for the first time. As he stops to inspect the sign with his name on it, a key light comes up on the letters and sets them glowing like the pride inside him. Much of the subjective sensation in an instance like this depends less on a formal manipulation than on a sustained identification with the character. The wedding night, though Will's painful self-consciousness is heightened by such things as the 'fweeping' sound of the bedroom door, is basically a silent exposition of his emotion rather than an externalization of it; and yet it is easy to feel embarrassment *with* him, as he arranges his starched collar front and cuffs on the mantelpiece or fumbles awkwardly out of his pants.

The most overtly 'directed' engagements of the camera are keyed to Hobson's drunk scenes. His falling movement upstairs at the film's start is a good illustration: it hurtles back from him in high angle medium shot as he trips rapidly up each step. At Moonrakers, after Maggie's departure, wide angle medium close shots accentuate Hobson's tipsy swaying; then the camera itself staggers to and fro with him as he gropes his way out. An occurrence of *delirium tremens* features a number of fantasy point-of-view shots. A swarm of imaginary locusts descending onto the bed and a man-sized grey mouse grinning over the footboard are intercut with reaction shots of Laughton squirming in his long-johns. The sight of one of his drinking companions sticking out his tongue in the mirror instead of Hobson's own reflection is composed over-shoulder, reinforcing the reality of it for the hallucination's victim and helping build to his climactic yell as he drops a pitcher of wash water.

For all the accuracy of its dialect and period characterizations, for all its drunks and slapstick moments, *Hobson's Choice* is not a standard, middle-country farce centered on the title's dilemma of having to take what's offered or nothing. This is partly because of its exploration of themes of social relationships and personal maturation. It is also because of Lean's additions and extrapolations. A scene like Hobson's alcohol-addled pursuit of the moon's reflection is a tour-de-force of comic surrealism. Lean develops it precisely: from Laughton's first quizzical glances, while leaning against a traditional lamppost, at the rippling likeness in the water; as he pulls up his trouser legs and hops after it from puddle to puddle like an oversized frog; to his antics below Beenstock and Son's window, unwaringly circling the open trap to the grain cellar. With the tremulous chords of Arnold's 'moon theme' on the track, Lean moves from the humorously absurd image of Laughton on his back with his feet caught on the guard chains and floundering like an overturned tortoise, to the chillingly eerie tumble down the grain shaft: a matte of Hobson, mouth gaping and eyes widened in surprise, over a forced perspective of bricks – the moon still looming unnaturally overhead after the body has dropped from sight, its theme sounding a note of final victory over the crash landing.

Hobson's Choice is not a simple comedy. It is truest to the inward direction of its personages and does not sacrifice that for the sake of laughter. Within that context, as serio-comedy, it relates most directly to

127

Lean's other work and is, in fact, not too far removed from the semi-comic tragedies of his next effort.

Chapter 7

THE PASSIONATE FRIENDS (1949)
SUMMER MADNESS (1955)

> There come and go and come again in
> the sky the threatening clouds, the ethereal
> cirrus, the red dawns and
> glowing afternoons of that passion
> of love which is the source and
> renewal of being.
>
> *H. G. Wells,* Passionate Friends

MORE A TRANSITIONAL work than anything else, *The Passionate Friends* (1949) turned Lean back from Dickens and a wider world-view to the more restricted themes of Romantic fantasy and disillusionment, back momentarily from the period trappings of mid-Victorianism and its happy endings to contemporary settings and sadder conclusions.

The modernization of Wells' novel is, in itself, curious and somewhat revealing. For while *Passionate Friends* falls most conspicuously between *Brief Encounter* (four years earlier) and *Summer Madness* (six years later), with Mary Justin forging a clear link between the former's Laura Jesson to the latter's Jane Hudson (all three characters have a love affair which becomes the focal point and is concluded concurrently with each film; but while Laura remains faithful out of continuing love for her husband, Mary Justin's marriage is one of convenience, and Jane is a spinster), it also anticipates *Madeleine,* on a direct (it was made immediately prior to it; both pictures star Ann Todd) and thematic level. Wells' original story was a combination epistle and first person history (written by its protagonist, Stephen Stratton, for his son and tracing events before the turn of the century to 1911), which explored, much as Lean would in *Madeleine,* rigid social conventions; and these are the real antagonists to the human figures in both novel and film. The movie's Mary Justin becomes, along with Madeleine Smith, the most unstable of Lean's heroines. Vacillating, as Madeleine would, between passion and a union for purely material satisfaction, Mary Justin (in the novel) is also driven to murder – in this instance, her own, but still the most extreme of solutions (and one also considered momentarily by a distraught Laura Jesson). While she is dissuaded from the attempt at the end of the screen version, much of the compulsive, increasingly schizophrenic behavior that drove her to suicide in Wells' conception remains.

Passionate Friends was Lean's first picture with Ann Todd (who was to replace Kay Walsh in his personal life as well as in his films). It is the first *and* last time that he would emphasize the qualities which caused her to be dubbed 'the English Garbo,' the cool, distended expressions and whispery voice he would deliberately play against in *Madeleine.* For part of the underlying normalcy of the other heroines, even at the height of their fantasies, is in their physical aspect. The wide-eyed, tweedy Laura Jesson and the energetic, accident-prone Jane Hudson with her constant 'Oh golly's' and 'Wow's' contrast markedly with the expensive wardrobe and aristocratic manner of Mary Justin. Even in everyday surroundings, Lean catches her wistfully contemplating in the moody sidelight of a bed lamp or aerily resplendent in evening gown and veil, makes her the most pictorially attractive of his women.

There is a consequential and problematic dichotomy in *Passionate Friends.* At times, it recaptures the glistening black-and-white compositions of the period films; the action, which derives from an intricate flashback plot development, and characterizations become melodramatically stylized. At other moments, though, particularly in the scenes with Steven Stratton – who, as played by Trevor Howard, is a literal re-in-carnation of Alec Harvey – Lean may verge back past the realistic, middle-class romance of *Brief Encounter* all the way (with the flashbacks of Mary before her marriage, girlishly holding hands in her ruffled print dress and lying next to Steven in the grass) to the juvenile love of Shorty and Freda in *In Which We Serve.* This bi-focal style is appropriate to Mary's own indecisiveness. As do Emile L'Angelier and William Minnoch, Stratton and Justin appeal to divergent aspects of the heroine's personality; but – more in the manner of Alec Harvey and Fred Jesson (even Jesson's name resembles 'Howard Justin') – the associations are less absolute, less polarized between rapturous abandon and dull security.

There are, however, inconsistencies in Mary's character which are never resolved. By evading the possibility of Mary's death (a possibility which the previous narrative has at least suggested if not firmly established), the conclusion compromises her. She returns to her husband vindicated neither by innocence (to face his unfounded accusations) nor by overwhelming strength of passion. It is difficult to speculate on why Wells' ending was abandoned. (Not is it fair to give the impression that the novel is faithfully adhered to in all other respects: the entire focus of the story shifts from Stratton to Mary, and the events are recounted in the context of her life rather than his). The film, as it is, neither follows through on Laura's rush to the edge of the tracks in *Brief Encounter* nor fully anticipates the ordeal of *Madeleine.* And while an analogy which would find Madeleine Smith parting amicably with L'Angelier and settling down with Minnoch is not entirely justifiable neither is it wholly farfetched.

The imagery of Mary and Steven's last idyll in the mountains clearly reflects back to the excursions into the countryside in *Brief Encounter.* The sequence in which they go boating on an Alpine lake might almost be match cut with a similar outing in *Summer Madness.* But the strongest

131

resemblance is one of basic attitudes on a character level. Mary Justin's remark, 'I want to belong to myself,' gives voice to an aspiration held in common with Madeleine Smith, but not with Laura Jesson, Jane Hudson, or even Maggie Hobson. Maggie's forceful pragmatism and Jane's career-woman status (which she is not above deprecating: 'Oh, [I'm just] a fancy secretary, really.') are partially, at best, consequences of their search for personal liberation. But more importantly, they are actively (Maggie) and passively (Jane) aimed at fulfilling or facilitating the realization of essentially romantic notions. The self-assessments of Mary ('I'm a hard woman') and Madeleine ('I do not regret things'), though, reflect an awareness of individual identity which will hold up under stress. The failure of their respective relationships arises from a struggle to maintain that awareness within a repressive social order, an order which throws their desires for love and independence into conflict.

Lean has frequently employed a narrative framework which, if not an actual series of flashbacks (as from the raft in *In Which We Serve*), is triggered by a movement backwards in time (as from 'T. E. Shaw's' funeral in *Lawrence of Arabia*). Often he has exploited the technique for novel or revealing effects (Yegraf's third-person voiceovers during scenes from his memory in *Doctor Zhivago* or the subjective 'replay' of the parting in *Brief Encounter*); but nowhere is it more compounded – and, perhaps, confounded – than in *Passionate Friends*. The meetings of Steven and Mary, separated by several years, might be viewed as an elaboration on a conversation in *Brief Encounter* (Laura: 'You think we shall ever see each other again?' Alec: 'I don't know. Not for years anyway.'). The scenes of their affair before her marriage – which Mary recalls after their first re-encounter – becomes a flurry of brief events, a montage reminiscent of Laura Jesson's romantic musings while gazing out the window of her train compartment and part of an abbreviated process of selective, almost fanciful remembering by Mary. But the overall structure, with overlapping flashbacks forming an episodic yet static (in terms of change) narrative, seems more analogous to Wells' 'threatening clouds [that] come and go and come again.' Most of the film drifts aimlessly, the past strung our like a ridge of hazy clouds interlaced with a present that may threaten but never bursts into dramatic intensity.

The climactic and central sequences in the Alps are part of the film's most consistent imagery. The lovers' last day together in the mountains completes the cycle which began in the natural settings of rural England. In the novel, a supporting character, representing societal judgment of the illicit affair, advises Stratton to stop being 'romantic and uncivilized.' The same values, the same antipathy between civilized behavior and unbridled ardor holds true in the movie. The final progression from Mary on a snow-capped peak with Steven to the white-tiled subway with Justin represents a movement away from the natural into the artificial, away from precarious independence towards conformity, back into what Henry James called 'a full-fed material insular world, a world of hideous florid plate and ponderous order and thin conversation.' It is equally a regression from a natural height (of passion – an image transposed from Wells) to an artificial subterranean depth (of repression – a striking extension of the original's direction). But again the film backs away from intensity. Relieved of the burden of Mary's suicide, the ending is, in various ways, Lean's most ambiguous – in terms of what will happen 'after' – and most realistic – in the sacrifice of sensation for security. It is also his least satisfactory: an abrupt change of course, an alternate conclusion as difficult as that of *Great Expectations* without its redeeming amplitude.

*   *   *   *   *

Summer Madness (1955) occupies a clear middle position in Lean's career. Between the black-and-white period pictures and the color/-widescreen productions of later years, it is, to date, his last contemporary film.* While not his initial effort in color, it is the first photographed

---

* An argument might be made for *Bridge on the River Kwai* or *Doctor Zhivago;* but none of the latter's screen time (except for fifteen minutes or so of the framing sequence at the dam) is contemporary. *Kwai,* while only dating back to the last World War, recreates, in its geographic isolation, an even more primitive setting.

Passionate Friends

The *'Passionate friends'* of the title – Mary Justin (Ann Todd) and Steven Stratton (Trevor Howard) share a drink. The film was released in the United States under the title *One Woman's Story.*

Above: Mary Justin (Ann Todd) and Miss Layton (Betty Ann Davies).

Below: Mary Justin (Ann Todd) and Steven Stratton (Trevor Howard) enjoy a chance meeting at an Alpine resort.

entirely on location – particular values which Lean has refused to abandon since. (When not working, Lean has even made the setting of *Summer Madness*, Venice, his adopted home). For the first time also, both his principal actors (Katharine Hepburn and Rossano Brazzi) and the source material (Arthur Laurents' play) were non-English. It was, in short, Lean's first step away from being a British director of British pictures aimed at a predominantly home audience towards becoming an international filmmaker working with 'foreign' producers and stars in a world market with all the attendant promise of swelling professional reputation and popular recognition.

Thematically, though, *Summer Madness* has much in common with its antecedents in Lean's work. Again, the imaginings of Laura Jesson aboard the train are an obvious referent. In *Summer Madness* the locale itself is anticipated by her dream image of riding with Alec Harvey in a gondola on the Grand Canal. The city of Venice is cast in a major role in *Summer Madness* – the film begins with her arrival and ends with her departure. The opening scene on the train:

ENGLISH PASSENGER:
Is this your first visit to Venice?

JANE:
Yes. Is it yours?

PASSENGER:
No, I've been here several times.

JANE: (mildly astonished)
Several times? You have!

PASSENGER:
Yes. I hope you're going to like it.

JANE:
Like it? I've got to. I've come such a long way.
I've saved up such a long time for this trip.
Do you think I, maybe, won't like it?

PASSENGER: (reassuring)
I'm sure you will. Not everybody likes it the
same way ... but the majority find it very
beautiful.

JANE: (still a bit apprehensive)
Yeah. Well, I guess I'll settle with the
majority.

reveals something about Venice, something about Jane, and something about the invisible 'majority' which will, as in the stories of Laura Jesson, Mary Justin, and Madeleine Smith, play its own part. The obvious analogies between Jane Hudson and these others have already been drawn. Yet in her particular way, Jane is a more *refined* and less *defined* characterization (closer in shared traits, if not in time, to Rosy Ryan). The admixture of opposing qualities makes her outgoing yet repressed, eager but anxious, brash yet self-conscious, graceful but a bit clumsy: she is sharply delineated and outwardly a most realistic figure (in the stage sense of 'drawn from life'). But few of the events of her past and little of her present occupation, almost nothing of her personal history is specified; and inwardly she is as much if not more prone to fantasy as any Lean heroine.

Jane is not 'put into context.' Her encounter with Venice is a dual synthesis of the everyday with the extraordinary – not just of the Romantic city with the plain American tourist but also of the commonplace streets and shops with the unusually romantic girl. ('In America every female under fifty calls herself a "girl".'). For all its directness of plot – there are no flash-backs in *Summer Madness;* it is restricted in terms of place and Jane's week-long stay – the film's action seems suspended in time while that synthesis takes place. It is, as the title suggests, a slightly delirious idyl momentarily detached from any simple progression of days on a calendar while Jane searches for 'what she's been missing all her life.'

That synthesis also involves coming to distinguish surface values from genuine ones, material experience from emotional. Just as Jane's notion of postcard Venice is gradually undermined (she pauses to take in a gondola drifting on a glistening canal to the strains of a distant serenade only to have her view temporarily obstructed by garbage being thrown into the water), so are her personal illusions about herself and others. Both the Jaegers and the McIlhennys aid in this process. The ostensibly happy, younger Eddie and Phyl Jaeger are not really the ideal couple Jane imagines – which realization distresses her most because it upsets her scheme of things. On a more figurative level, Jaeger, the painter, Phyl with an art book under her arm trying to understand his work, even the methodical Lloyd McIlhenny – who despite his timetables ('Independent activity – we're allowed two hours of it every day') and crass remarks ('To me it's just Luna Park on water') is impressed by the museum ('That place certainly sold me Art. That you gotta see, Miss Hudson') – are all caught up in a superficial, two-dimensional world with no more substance than a landscape. Jane herself looks at the city through the viewfinder of her camera. The compulsion she has with it is introduced in the first scene: 'Oh, boy, Gotta get a shot of this [the lagoon]. Oh, golly! Fifth one of these I've used already. Haven't even got there yet.' On film, she reduces the world to two-dimensions, until it becomes, as in McIlhenny's comment of the art museum: 'hundreds of pictures, all done by hand,' not only something she can possess, can take home and see again, but also a reality which she can selectively manipulate screening out the discordant sights and even titling it (she has the English passenger on the train hold a travel brochure for 'Venice – City of Romance' while she photographs it). The camera is a tool for creating that 'romance' and an habitual sublimation, the value of which Jane must re-assess during the course of the film.

Materially, the red goblet and the white gardenia are more important, more varied symbols than the camera. Like her home movies they are souvenirs; but they are also tangible, three-dimensional objects. And they are central to Jane's understanding of her situation. For whether the goblet she buys from Renato is truly an Eighteenth century antique or one like the half-dozen others purchased by the McIlhennys at the glass works is another superficial consideration. The valuation, the appreciation of people is not. The gardenia is a remnant of schoolgirl dreams:

RENATO:
Why did you choose that flower?

JANE:
I once went to a ball. Not just
an ordinary dance, but a real ball. It was the
first one I'd ever been to. Somehow I'd got it
into my mind that I had to wear a gardenia. I
don't know why. I guess I'd read about
gardenias in a book or something. I must have
– I didn't even know what they were.

RENATO:
And did you wear one?

JANE:
Gardenias turned out to cost two dollars
apiece; and the boy I was going with was still
in college. But it was a nice dream.

RENATO:
Well, now you have your gardenia.

JANE:
Yes.

RENATO:
Everything happens sooner or later.

JANE:
Yeah, that's what they say. Everything happens
to him who waits . . .

Like the film itself, the elements in this scene alternate between those dreams and actuality. The dialogue lingers over the illogical, youthful wish and the rich associations of 'not just ordinary' ballrooms, while violins in the background play 'Summertime in Venice' (a song linked with the couple throughout the picture – almost an archetypal underscoring as was the Rachmaninoff concerto in *Brief Encounter*). But pragmatic necessities dispel her dream. And as the physically present Renato supersedes the memory of the 'boy,' Jane becomes anxious, falls back into conversational generalities and subtly dodges any kind of involvement – as with the use of an impersonal 'him' rather than a more affirmative 'her' in the last line.

Both the goblet and the flower bring up the question of Jane's willingness to trust others, to risk becoming involved. For that question and the answers found in the affair with Renato are the film's major concern. There is an initial explicitness which can leave little doubt about what Jane wants; but her guardedness, her way of talking about 'a girl on the boat coming over' rather than herself to Signora Fiorina:

> JANE: (by the balcony of her room)
> Way back, way back in the back of her mind
> was something she was looking for.
>
> SIGNORA FIORINA:
> What?
>
> JANE: (spreading her arms out over the city)
> A wonderful, magical, mystical miracle!
>
> FIORINA:
> No? To do what?
>
> JANE: (after a moment's hesitation) Beats me.

and her cynical remark at the end, all suggest that the greatest hindrance to finding her 'miracle,' what really 'beats her,' is her own insecurity. Unlike Mary Justin or Maggie Hobson, heroines inclined to take a more active part in the resolution of their desires, Jane just spreads her arms out over the city and waits.

140

The subjectification in *Summer Madness* is certainly not as pervasive as in *Brief Encounter* – nor, operating from a different plot referent, should it be – but Lean does employ the technique to expose Jane's sensations at the *pensione*. Contrasting with the exultant stance on the balcony against the bright, sunlit city is a later medium shot of Jane in her full white dress sitting on her bed amid the dark grey and brown furnishings of the room, posed contemplatively like a Vermeer figure (a pose reinforced with the added dimension of the scrape of slippers on the floor, the distant clanging of a single bell, and the canal water lapping against wooden hulls outside – selected sounds of isolation). The scene of Jane alone on the terrace – pacing back and forth, listening to the street singers and the lovers laughing, throwing a rock into the water to break the tension only to retreat in embarrassment when a gondolier mistakes it for a summons – is the most subjectively expressive (made to seem genuinely poignant rather than heavy-handed when she is brought to the brink of tears); and is less manipulative or contrived than a later scene with the Jaegers when Jane, after failing in earlier exhortations to have them join her in a drink ('Prego, pretty prego'), asks to accompany them on their evening out: by holding on the couple in the boat after Jane has given up and withdrawn back onto the terrace out of sight, Lean reveals their hesitation to the audience but not to her, slipping momentarily and effectively into the ironic mode and diminishing identification with her subjective emotion when he cuts back up to her.

Throughout Lean drives the picture forward from these small, climactic moments when Jane is flustered or embarrassed. By restructuring in this fashion, he not only moves away from the rhetorical, thematic explicitness of the play but also provides a dynamic flow between what were originally static acts and scenes. (An idea of how complete the adaptation is may be given by noting that all of the play's action was confined to the terrace and sitting room). The failings of *This Happy Breed* and *Blithe Spirit* are not in evidence – and the reason is the nature of Jane Hudson, a nature not found in the Gibbons or Condomine households.

141

Summer Madness

Renato leaves Jane (Katharine Hepburn) alone in the sitting room, still somewhat in doubt as to whether she has been deceived or not. A scene from *"Summer Madness"*.

ove: Katharine Hepburn as Jane Hudson.

low: Jane Hudson (Katharine Hepburn) and Mauro (Gaitano Audiero).

Although the key to Jane's emotional flux, her self-consciousness renders her a more physically expressive figure than Laura Jesson or Mary Justin, there is not really much comic effect derived from it in the sense of making her actions something to laugh at. In fact, there is little in *Summer Madness* to qualify it as comedy neither in the traditional sense of a 'happy ending' nor with an abundance of amusing scenes, little except wry asides – such as the gondola jam created by the weekend tourists as 'Santa Lucia' plays and loudspeakers recommend a glance at 'page 27 of your guidebooks.' The terrace scenes have more an air of desperate pathos than comedy; and Jane's acute discomfort on discovering the other goblets flares out in anger rather than awkwardness, so that her tipping over the chair becomes intensely dramatic, particularly following the banter of the departing McIlhennys.

The fall into the canal is a good example of a scene fulfilling several functions simultaneously. On a narrative level, it supplies the needed excuse for Di Rossi to call immediately upon Jane at the Hotel (politely inquiring if she is all right); it is also comic action, a restatement of a stock gag (Jane losing her footing while backing up to get a picture of Di Rossi's shop). Lean also combines the subjective factor of having the audience share another disconcerting moment with Jane (perhaps the severest in the film) with the ironic presence of Mauro (unable to get a word in and resigned to watching helplessly) and prolongs the pure comedy of the scene by having an unidentified witness perform a replay for his friends (but in high angle long shot rather than the more engaging, eye-level medium shot of Jane) up to and including the tumble into the water. This both extends the laughter and, while Jane is off-screen, allows for a gradual dissipation of the viewer's empathetic embarrassment. Finally, the sequence links the camera to Jane's 'loss of control' – a physical loss of equilibrium in the action itself and an implied emotional agitation underscored by her feeble quip about 'trying out for the Olympics,' as she slips through the crowd and hurries away fearful of Di Rossi coming out and seeing her.

That link begins in the very first scene with Di Rossi, where, characteristically, Lean provides a visual summary of the inner states of both protagonists. Jane sits at an outdoor table near San Marco: while idly photographing the passers-by she inadvertently records a pick-up. For the first time her selective control of the scene is disrupted; her personal view of Venice is intruded upon. Disturbed, she stops filming; while she rewinds (in medium close shot, foreground), a pan reveals Di Rossi seated behind her reading a paper (medium shot, background). Lean holds on the continuing action (she raises the camera to her eye and resumes; the motor noise catches his attention) then inserts a shot of some flags (seen through her viewfinder) drifting langourously in the breeze, which sets-up (after a medium close of him now intent on Jane) Di Rossi's close point-of-view of the folds of her dress, fluttering over her legs, moving up to her waist. The intensity of his gaze is translated into a track to a close-up of the back of her head; she senses it, fumbles with her sunglasses in symbolic concealment, and the incident ends.

The conflicting impulses which Lean sets in motion here are not quite the same as those of *The Passionate Friends*. An instructive contrast may be possible using Vittorio De Sica's *Stazione Termini* [*Indiscretion Of An American Wife (1952)*]. Like *Passionate Friends* this film opposes impulsive physical attraction to the guilt of acting contrary to established morality (by engaging in an adulterous affair). It is also analogous to *Summer Madness* in that it considers the same cultural differences which finally separate Jane and Di Rossi (American woman, Italian lover) and operates within the same restrictions of time and place (a few days in Venice; a few hours in a Roman train station). It differs because Jane is never guilty except in the most puritanical sense – she and Renato are never forced (by society or by the Motion Picture Code) to conclude that what they are doing is wrong. The cause of her repression, as has been noted, is less from fear of social judgment than from personal insecurity and unwillingness to 'be hurt,' presumably again. De Sica's picture is shot almost completely in interiors, full of shadowy compositions, oppressively tight close two-shots, and lonely figures framed against dark metallic objects and modern glass fixtures or caught in crowds. Lean, on the other

145

hand, has no choice but to energetically open up the play. He must find architectural expanses for his long shots, must concentrate on daylit exteriors and fill the nights with fireworks or music by Rossini, must, in order to discover the magic that Jane expects from the 'City of Romance,' to make the miracle possible, provide a landscape that encourages her to free and instinctive responses.

The subsequent scenes between Jane and Di Rossi are increasingly stylized. The second encounter, where Jane's eye is caught by Di Rossi's red goblet in the shop window much as his ear was caught by the noise of her camera, is a partial reversal of the first – she doesn't look up and recognize him until after she has removed her sunglasses. But their interaction is still mannered, not spontaneous, with the artificiality on Jane's part emphasized when she returns to the cafe on the chance of seeing him again, pretends to be with someone, and unwittingly discourages him when he does pass by. Later, Lean will exploit two long sections of theatrical dialogue, adding dramatic tension by staging both not just in long takes but in medium close two shots subliminally accentuated by slow, almost imperceptible travelling in's – a motion which both seems to bring the couple closer together in a diminishing frame and parallels the gradual development, from basic lines of communication to greater frankness and finally understanding, in their dialogue. As Jane's facade is penetrated and her demuring assaulted by Renato, as she is awakened emotionally, Lean changes pace again with his compositions and editing. The progression from the discussion of gardenias during the evening concerts and Jane's hushed 'I love you' after Di Rossi kisses her (mostly in medium shots) to an overhead extra long shot of her crossing a crowded square (with her tiny figure moving in such a way that the reading time for the shot is unusually short) reflects her growing animation, which is sustained in the succeeding montage of buying accessories and visiting the beauty parlor and restated in the dance scenes that evening.

The last additional element is color. There are overtly symbolic usages as in Jane's mute admission of the goblet's catalytic role reflected in the

146

red dress she wears in a later scene. But primarily color contributes greater pictorial expressiveness to Jane's passionate evolution. It first changes from the dull brown and trapped, hazy sunlight between the two-shot in the parlor (when Jane's hair is still wet and wrapped in a towel from her accident) to the deep blue outside Renato's house (the only light when he pursues her, in evening clothes, down a dark alleyway). Then, after the explosions of fireworks bathing them in multi-colored flashes as they embrace on the balcony, the final, immutable hues of the houses on the 'Isle where the Rainbow fell' and their tranquil pose against the fiery colorations of the setting sun in an open sky (like Wells' 'glowing afternoon of passion') mark the completion of a cycle, the end of Jane's transformation and the resolution of her inner conflict.

The bursts from the skyrockets also function (almost exactly like the longer and better-known sequence in Hitchcock's *To Catch A Thief* [1955]) as sexual images which are among Lean's most direct and explicit. He may have chosen to drive the point home with such literal explosiveness simply as part of the generally vivid scheme of imagery. But it might be more impressionistically interpreted as a celebration of the fact that, to that point in his work, more than any other character adapted from play or novel, Jane Hudson is Lean's character. Lean alters not just the name but, with Katharine Hepburn, her whole way of being, her appearance (Laurents' Leona Samish was played on Broadway by Shirley Booth) *and* her attitude. From the first glimpse of her on the train crossing the lagoon, she is no longer a cynical, intemperate, slightly overweight, middle-aged woman running away from life, but one who somehow senses that she has missed something and is energetically running after it. Leona Samish loses because she can never accept life for what it is, never come to grips with the problem that (as Phyl Jaeger tells her) 'everybody loves you,' but no *one* loves you; Jane wins because she can.

In Renato Di Rossi and in the use of Rossano Brazzi, Lean creates a male lead distinctly different from the earlier Trevor Howard parts. Despite his protest, in character, about being an 'ordinary man,' there is

147

no way to avoid – even in playing against Brazzi's 'Latin lover' image – some connotation lodged in his physical aspect of storybook prince coming to fulfil schoolgirl dreams. Of course, it might be slightly inappropriate, given the visual context Lean creates with Venice, for Jane Hudson to discover anyone else; it would definitely be incongrous for Alec Harvey to swab the salt spray from her eye while waiting for a gondola. The Di Rossi of *Time of the Cuckoo* is something of a gigolo, careless with his money at best, unscrupulous at worst, Lean makes Di Rossi almost painfully sincere, for Lean's interest, obviously, is in the fantasy/reality of Jane's world, in the way *she,* and no one else, deceives herself. Accordingly, Di Rossi becomes an honest, stable, and mature figure, not just in quantitative years of age but also in qualitative light of Lean's other pictures. Lean is still playing against both the anxieties of social codes of conduct and wearying worldly outlooks (as represented in Fiorina's remark about her former lover: 'For several years now we've been ... unexcited.'), still essentially realist in characterization, and still some distance temporally and tempermentally from Andrew Doryan in *Ryan's Daughter.* Di Rossi is not, it turn's out, Jane's storybook prince – just an antique dealer who speaks humorously imperfect English ('He is my niece') and challenges her more prudish romantic pre-conceptions with bizarre similes ('You are hungry . . . eat the ravioli'). And because he is, it becomes possible in the final scenes, in a way it never was before, for Jane to 'eat the ravioli,' for her to separate fantasy from reality, for her to realize happily as Renato runs after her train that the physical possession of the gardenia, the fulfilment of the dream, is less valuable than the unguarded emotional experience.

Chapter 8

THE BRIDGE ON THE RIVER KWAI (1957)

Up with me; up with me into the clouds!
For thy song, Lark, is strong;
Up with me, up with me into the clouds!
Singing, singing,
With clouds and sky about thee ringing,
Lift me, guide me till I find
That spot which seems so much to my mind!

William Wordsworth,
'To a Skylark'

'I LIKE DOING films in rather wild places. I find wild places exciting.'
Lean's love affair with exotic locations really begins with *The Bridge on the River Kwai.* In Ceylon and, in later ventures, in the Jordanian desert and on the desolate West Coast of Ireland, Lean forges visual correlatives to his personal excitement. But as he devotes himself more and more to such location shooting, his time in production also increases. The one year spent on *Bridge on the River Kwai* will mushroom into the three year gestation periods for *Lawrence of Arabia, Doctor Zhivago,* and *Ryan's*

149

Daughter. Admittedly, some of these projects were of an epic scale that would justify if not demand such an expenditure of time; but there was always more to it than that. Lean himself admits that 'making a film does get to be a drug for me. . . once started, it's hard for me to stop.' And it is no secret that after a year of filming *Lawrence of Arabia,* Sam Spiegel had to 'drag' Lean out of the Jordanian desert. This desire to extend the experience of the film for as long as possible suggests the more compulsive side of Lean's particular artistry. In the face of this, it is, again, difficult to understand how many can accuse him of detachmemt. If anything, his films are, to quote Strelnikov in *Doctor Zhivago,* 'absurdly personal.'

Bridge on the River Kwai can actually be divided into two pictures: one a story of personal conflicts (the Nicholson-Saito confrontation), the other a stereotyped, quasi-cynical action piece (the Shears 'adventure'). They are even divided geographically for most of the film, only coming together in the first and final sequences. The opening shot is that of a hawk soaring above the jungle. This free spirit, this archetypal symbol of the 'soul of man,' provides immediate contrast with the prisoner of war camp, where the men's spirits are far from free. In a crude graveyard, two men are burying one of their comrades. One of them is Shears: a cynical, arrogant American who masquerades as an officer, buys his way out of work (with shiny items taken from corpses), and laments over his compatriots' graves like a parody of a Greek chorus ('Here lies Corporal Herbert Thompson, serial number 01234567, valiant member of the King's own, or Queen's own, or something.'). His announced goals are simply staying alive and, eventually, escaping the compound.

William Holden, who plays Shears, is confidently at home in this part. Throughout the late Forties and early Fifties he was frequently cast in this type of role (most notably in Billy Wilder's *Stalag 17*), coming to represent to many Europeans the quintessential, somewhat ugly American. Typical of these Holden characterizations was an exaggerated, sarcastic disregard for others, frequently nullified by a final, out-of-character act of mercy. *Bridge* is no exception: after carefully establishing

150

his disenchantment with the world in general and his abhorrence of both war and heroics, Shears becomes a conventional hero at the end by saving Major Warden and sacrificing his life to complete his mission (destroying the bridge). Shears' 'Why me?' is never satisfactorily answered; but to contemporary audiences the act of questioning made him the center of the film, the character most easily understood and discussed. Repeated viewings, however, may suggest a lack of real interest on Lean's part in Shears' story. In fact, the only redeeming (in Lean's eyes) and believable (in the spectator's eyes) quality Shears has is his desire to survive. Not only does he refuse to accept the half-death of the prison (where, ironically, he is the chief gravedigger), but he speaks of following his instincts and the importance of living to the fullest. Visually, the colorful wreath of flowers given him by the natives or the yellow tie he dons when escaping the prison are Lean's familiar shorthand for dynamism. But beyond these few, disparate images, on a character level, the director's actual concentration is on the story of the two enemy Colonels 'locked' into this isolated jungle camp.

The conflict of Colonels Nicholson (the newly-arrived English POW) and Saito (the Japanese commandant) is constructed on a series of dualities, drawn for two purposes: first, to make the rather banal social point that enemies in war are only superficially different (despite propaganda to the contrary); second and more descriptively, to place them within the same psychological and spiritual sphere. In many of the wide-screen compositions of the two men, they are, though at opposite ends of the frame, in similar positions. In their initial confrontation in the prison yard, each is placed in a military posture with his men behind him (the stiff-upper-lip Nicholson to the right of frame; the overbearing Saito to the left). At the Colonels' two conferences over a table, this opposition continues (with Saito now on the right); and Saito's first formal meeting with his officers is composed analogously to Nicholson's council with his own men. Up to and including the final scene at the river, the visual parallels are precisely drawn.

Further, on a narrative level, each antagonist accuses the other, on

151

separate occasions, of madness. But the most obvious plot link between them is simply the profession and rank which they hold in common and their attitude towards this occupation. Both Saito and Nicholson are servants of King (Emperor) and Country who execute orders and follow 'the book' (in this instance, for Saito, the imperial command to construct the bridge at any cost; for Nicholson, the Geneva Code for 'without law there is no civilization'). At first, their dispute seems no deeper than that – a clash of rule books – until Saito's decision to escalate it with the humiliating (or so it would be for him) experience of the sweat-box.

The first glimpse of Saito is in his hut – dressed in kimono and framed by Japanese prints and cherry blossoms. When he goes out to meet Nicholson and his company, he puts on a modern uniform but retains the traditional samurai sword. For Saito is very much a remnant (as were many Japanese officers) of the feudal Tokugawa period, a traditional warrior (Saito: [to Nicholson) 'You speak to me of code. What code? The coward's code. What do you know of the soldier's code? Of *bushido?*'). From a set of standards which has lasted generations, Saito's life derives a continuity with the past (with his ancestry) and a degree of meaning. It is his own 'escape from reality' (something he accuses the prisoners of) and his justification for fighting the war. Ultimately, this code is even more important than the war and can even supersede imperial orders (as when the doctor convinces Saito that it would violate his principles to shoot the unarmed English officers, although the massacre might have eliminated the resistance among the ranks to building the bridge). Everything about Saito, public and private, his expression, his carriage, the box he stands on to address assemblies in the yard – all are implements in what he understands to be a rigorous application of this code. And it is finally *bushido,* a loss of face after Nicholson has taken over and Saito been knocked off his soap-box, which will demand his ritual suicide (although it is abrogated by another's knife).

Nicholson's situation is slightly different: he has no ironclad, time-defying 'way of the warrior' to guide him. He follows, instead, the more informal standards of a professional soldier. His personal beliefs dictate

152

The Bridge On the River Kwai

ed Prisoners of war march across a bridge they built for the Japanese in *The Bridge on the River Kwai.*

Above: The confrontatio
Colonel Saito (Sessue
Hayakawa) and Colonel
Nicholson (Alec Guinne

Left: Colonel Saito (Ses
Hayakawa) in *The Bridg
on the River Kwai,* surve
work on the bridge.

ove: Colonel Nicholson (Alec Guinness) is victorious over Saito.

low: Colonel Nicholson's (Alec Guinness) death.

The end of *The Bridge on the River Kwai.*

discipline and strict obedience; and there is no doubt that Nicholson obeys like a 'maniac' (according to Shears' description). He suffers torture so that his officers will not have to work as promised by the Geneva Convention; moreover he refuses to acknowledge any inferiority in his position (engendering Saito's remark: 'I hate the English . . you are defeated but you have no shame. I hate the English.') retaining the unassailable advantage of stolid composure. But as the film progresses, Nicholson gradually strays from an authoritarian outlook and chooses to indulge some of his own fancies. The vision of erecting a bridge which will endure for hundreds of years compulsively fascinates and takes hold of him. After the work is completed, he reflects with Saito on its 'beauty:'

SAITO: (agreeing)
Yes, a beautiful creation.

NICHOLSON: (Leaning over a guardrail
                          as the sun sets)
I've been thinking. Tomorrow it will
be twenty-eight years to the day that
I've been in the service, twenty-
eight years in peace and war. I don't
suppose I've been home more than ten
months in all that time. . .

     [he changes position]

Still, it's been a good life. I
loved India. I wouldn't have had
it any other way. But there are
times when suddenly you realize you're
nearer the end than the beginning.
And you wonder. . . you ask yourself. . .
what the sum total of your life represents. What difference your being
there at any time made to anything.

157

Hardly made any difference at all,
really, particularly in comparison
with other men's careers. I don't
know whether that kind of thinking's
very healthy; but I must admit I've
had some thoughts on those lines from
time to time.

[joyfully]

But tonight. . . tonight!

For most of the monologue, Nicholson is seen from what might be interpreted as Saito's point-of-view (a tight medium shot at an angle from the back), eliciting Saito's empathy but not really engaging his understanding. To make his 'being there' count for something, Nicholson forfeits the very rights he would not allow violated earlier (his officers are put to work, the sick are impressed into service). Although the Doctor may wonder whether building a bridge for the enemy is treasonous or not, Nicholson is beyond consideration of the war or treason, of anything except realising his vision. It is his desperate attempt to contradict the Doctor's earlier observation that 'no one will ever know or care what happens to us.' Nicholson has become another John Ridgefield (in fact, similarly 'obsessive,' atonal chords accompany a travelling shot aboard a raft, as the Colonel relates his plan to his brother officers).

When the bridge is completed and a memorial plaque identifying builders is attached, Nicholson walks proudly over his monument and lovingly inspects it (pausing to pick up a stray nail which mars its aspect). Unknown to him, on the near shore are a group of more practical men (including Shears and Major Warden), men who make a battlefield out of a botanical garden, men who have come with cordite and plastique to annihilate his dream. With these destroyers also arrives Nicholson's final dilemma; which loyalty is greater? In Lean's original ending, the

Colonel consciously chose not to expose the commandoes and himself pushed the plunger which demolished the bridge. But (under pressure from the producers) an ambiguous conclusion was inserted, in which Nicholson is hit by shrapnel and falls on the plunger (thereby taking the decision out of his hands). Either way, the Romantic myth of perpetuating a personal identity vanishes like the plaque which floats down the river amid the debris. The Doctor, still in his role of observer, delivers a fitting eulogy: 'Madness! Madness!'

It is madness, the madness of men with distorted values, the madness of a distracted dreamer. But more than that it is the insanity of a combat which makes enemies of men with much in common; which compels tired and bleeding soldiers to march proudly into a prison camp; which can twist an ordinary, constructive act (the bridge) into an abnormal one; which in short, can inspire all the waste and destruction chronicled in *Bridge on the River Kwai.* The last shot of the film, like the first, is of a hawk flying over. Father Collins' caution to Rosy Ryan watching the gulls ('What are you expectin'? Wings, is it?') comes too late for a Nicholson, shattered, with his own wings broken.

> Alas! my journey, rugged and uneven,
> Through prickly moors or dusty ways must wind:
> But hearing thee, or others of thy kind,
> As full of gladness and as free of heaven,
> I, with my fate contented, will plod on,
> And hope for higher raptures, when life's day is done.

Chapter 9

LAWRENCE OF ARABIA (1962)

All men dream: but not equally. Those who
dream by night in the dusty recesses of their
minds wake in the day to find that it was
vanity: but the dreamers of the day are
dangerous men, for they may act their dream
with open eyes, to make it possible.

> *Thomas Edward Lawrence,*
> The Seven Pillars of Wisdom

We live, as we dream – alone,

> *Joseph Conrad,*
> The Heart of Darkness

LAWRENCE OF ARABIA is the beginning of the most impressive period of
Lean's career and, far from coincidentally, of his association with British
playwright Robert Bolt. Dissatisfied with Michael Wilson's sprawling
adaptation of the T. E. Lawrence story (based principally on *The Seven
Pillars of Wisdom),* Lean and Sam Spiegel began to search for someone
else, preferably someone with an ear for English intonation, to rework
the script. Favorably impressed by 'A Man for All Seasons,' they chose
Bolt.

The creative merger of Bolt's writing style, rooted in the traditional theater, and Lean's somewhat 'classical' approach to direction seemed perfect. As Bolt himself observes about his work: 'I tried. . . for a bold and beautiful verbal architecture,' a rough equivalent to the visual style which Lean had been fashioning for twenty years. In Bolt's work, symbols like the 'flowering cherry' in the play of the same name and the sea versus land imagery of 'A Man for All Seasons' reveal an ability to think in terms of visual metaphor and almost cinematic oppositions (Lean readily concedes that the cut from a match to the desert at sunrise in *Lawrence* was one of Bolt's conceptions).

> For [Thomas] More again the answer to this
> question would be perfectly simple (though
> again not easy); the English Kingdom, his
> immediate society, was subservient to the larger
> society of the Church of Christ, founded by
> Christ, extending over Past and Future, ruled
> from heaven. There are still some for whom
> that is perfectly simple, but for the most it can
> only be a metaphor. I took it as a metaphor of
> that larger context which we all inhabit, the
> terrifying cosmos. Terrifying because no laws,
> no sanctions, no mores apply there; it is either
> empty or occupied by God and Devil nakedly
> at war. The sensible man will seek to live his
> life without dealings with this larger
> environment, treating it as a fine spectacle on a
> clear night, or a subject for innocent curiosity.
> At the most he will allow himself an agreeable
> *frisson* when he contemplates his own relation
> to the cosmos, but he will not try to live in it;
> he will gratefully accept the shelter of his
> society. This was certainly More's intention.

162

In his preface to 'A Man for All Seasons' Bolt expresses the kind of cosmic sense, the notion of fulfilment of destiny, shared by Ridgefield in *The Sound Barrier* and Nicholson in *Bridge on the River Kwai.* Just as Lean's recurring images of birds in flight represent, in a visually succinct way, a desire for freedom, for escape from societal restrictions, Bolt's comments – 'Well, one answer [to their problems], the only answer, is that there is no human predicament. That is the Christian viewpoint. Because man does not belong to the earth. . .' – reveal a verbal understanding of this same human need. The discovery of individual destiny and its consequential, almost megalomaniac alienation – an awareness of which Lean and Bolt had independently developed – becomes Lawrence's great obsession in the film.*

This, rather than any discussion of the importance of Thomas Edward Lawrence, the figure in history, is the key to *Lawrence of Arabia,* the film. (For anyone so interested there is *The Seven Pillars of Wisdom* in which the adventurer himself philosophizes about his exploits in the desert.) But the historical presence of this man, the undersized bastard son of an English peer who went from leading armies to repairing airplanes for the R.A.F., is only a superficial concern for Lean and Bolt. They focus instead on the spiritual dimensions of an enigma; and, in this context, such wanderings from the historical path as the casting of the tall, handsome O'Toole in the lead (making him the spiritual rather than physical equivalent of Lawrence) are understandable. Within the framework of factual incident – World War I and the Arab-English drive against Axis Turkey – is presented a man who has chosen to descend not only into the primitive landscapes of the desert but also to venture through the dark terrain of his own mind. His long treks across endless expanses of sand parallel his recurrent withdrawals into Self, in order to search out his course of action, his roots, his primal identity. For the

---

*If one still has doubts about this shared pre-occupation, a comparison of the dreamer-hero of Bolt's *Flowering Cherry* with any number of Lean's heroes or heroines should provide ample evidence.

conflict between the blonde, fair-skinned 'Arab' and the slightly affected English officer, between El Aurens and Lawrence, between deliverer and demon is only a particularization of a long-standing inner conflict (General Murray; 'I cannot make out whether you're bloody bad mannered or just half-witted.' Lawrence: 'I have the same problem myself.'). What Lawrence ultimately aspires to be is never clear, not even to himself. But he longs for the desert, for the catharsis of heat that he merely toys with by snuffing out matches with his fingers, for a blistering purgatory (in the face of Dryden's warning that 'only Bedouins and gods get fun out of the desert. And you are neither.'). So to free himself from the parlor games of the intelligence service, where 'the trick is not minding it hurts,' and his own psychological snares, he enters the desert.

Lawrence quickly adapts to the desert *and* the Arabs. Simultaneously he becomes a dreamer of the day. The 'fact' that this Welshman is out of place here is never visualized. Rather Lean catches him reclining contemplatively in front of the bleached branches of a tangled, windswept bush. Already, with his dusty tan uniform and his sand-flecked hair and skin, he has begun to blend with the natural surroundings. Exteriorly his figure is camouflaged or lost in the panoramic long shots where Lawrence and his guide become specks in the desert tides. Internally he senses the beginning of something ('I am different' he assures Tafas), he discovers a latent destiny.

The first chance to test this is the encounter with Sherif Ali at the Harith well. Framed together at opposite edges of a medium shot, it is Ali, not Lawrence, who stands out from the background in his black robes, who dominates the frame. Yet it is Lawrence who seems to draw strength from the terrain, who despite the murder of his Masruh guide is confidently resilient, like the desert brush, against Ali's blustering threats ('You have no fear, English?' 'My fear is my concern.') It is the outsider who remains unperturbed before this dark, menacing figure who has slipped from the waves of a mirage to kill his friend, steal his compass, and perhaps leave him to perish. It is Ali who is a bit unnerved; and from the empty sky that remains when Ali has ridden out of the

164

frame, Lean tilts down to reveal Lawrence riding in the distance, tranquil and alone.

'I think you are another of these desert-loving English.' There is justice in King Feisal's observation; but the desert seems to reciprocate that love, the elements fall into accord around Lawrence. In a meeting with Feisal, Lawrence demonstrates a knowledge of those elements and of Arab tradition ('I think your book is right: the desert is an ocean in which no oar is dipped.') and a sympathy for both. But Feisal is direct and pragmatic: We need what no man can provide, Mr Lawrence. We need a miracle.' While he speaks, a mysterious night wind arises and the masts of the tent creak in response. As if hearing a deific message, Lawrence goes among the dunes to contemplate. Again his position is visually understated: a high angle shot flattens him against a wall of rippling sand, the thin form of a minor British functionary arrayed against the currents of natural and historical force. Lawrence ponders this dilemma through a night of wind and dust, wandering in long shot, until morning lights his crouching silhouette, and a close-up as he breathes the decision to himself: 'Akaba.'

Akaba, or Jerusalem, or Mecca – Lawrence pronounces it like a shrine. For in this scene of ordeal in the desert (in the creation of Feisal's 'Miracle'), Lean and Bolt begin to extend the image of a mortal facing personal cataclysm to include Messianic analogies and religious symbols. In all three collaborations *(Lawrence of Arabia, Doctor Zhivago,* and *Ryan's Daughter)* these crypto-religious allegories re-inforce the image of the hero as a man striving to be apart from others and/or to affect a scheme of destiny. Although the success of Lean and Bolt's characters in realizing these goals is usually limited, the human agonies and joys of pursuing the ideal can assume mythic proportions – proportions which are particularly apt in Lawrence's case: that of a man aspiring like Moses or Christ or Mohammed to lead and prophesy.

The deific equation is established in the initial cut from Dryden's office to the desert. In an instant, the artifacts (an alabaster Egyptian cat, a painting of a sunrise), the artificial is left behind. That sentiment is echoed in Lawrence's action, in the more natural blowing out of the match rather than extinguishing it with his fingers. But beyond the obvious meanings of the cut (the painting is animated, another layer of reality is embodied in an expanded 'frame') and the timing of it to the match going out (Lawrence no longer needs to sustain himself with match games when he has the limitless heat of the sun), the sun itself appears suddenly on the right of the frame exactly where Lawrence was standing. Whether it replaces him or he becomes it, the implications of a fiery inner rising or of a new Ra being born are unobstrusively added.

After this, after the Apocalyptic image of the golden solar disc shimmering through the silent curtain of heat, Lawrence begins to assume dimensions that are larger than life. He does so literally when he clambers awkwardly up onto his camel and, in extension of the archetypal parallels, 'Full of the Holy Spirit. . . [is] led by the Spirit about the desert for forty days.' (Luke 4:1-2) Whether Lawrence resists or assimilates the power of the desert does not qualify or diminish the experience, the ordeal of his own 'forty days' gaining knowledge in the wilderness. He does assimilate, but Lean does not disguise his figure to the point of making him just an animated shrub or bit of rock – that would go counter to the direction already indicated. From the earliest scenes Lawrence is associated with wind, speed, fire, heat, and light. All these suggest a pantheistic union with the elements, but none erase the individuality of Lawrence.

Mentally, Lawrence's delusions are not of grandeur. Before entering Feisal's camp, he emerges purified. Although there may be a reflection of expanding self-esteem behind the comic relief of his singing 'I'm the Man who broke the bank at Monte Carlo' and listening for the echo, the principal connotations are of a kind of spiritual rapture. More importantly, Brighton's applause, which reverberates over shot like a series of distant gunshots, and the contrast to Lawrence he affords in his impeccable uniform re-affirm the ominous presence of a 'real' world, a world at war which summons Lawrence back to his 'public life.' So when the despondent Feisal looks around in the midst of a Turkish air raid a

166

point-of-view reveals Lawrence behind the black smoke, suddenly before him in medium close shot, as if risen from the earth in answer to his prayers.

Lawrence's second confrontation with Sherif Ali comes after his night of meditation, and this time he is clearly the victor. In a sustained close two shot, the dark and light faces contend within the restricted frame – separated in mind over the feasibility of crossing the Nefud desert and in body (in two dimensions) by the mast of the tent – until a cut back gives Lawrence room to raise his arm decisively and exclaim: 'It's only a matter of going.' Lawrence's fervor (Ali calls it madness), overwhelms any reluctance or apprehension; he acquires disciples (the gap-toothed Gasim; the eager Farraj and Daud who kiss his feet and receive blows for him, causing Ali to remark: 'These are not servants. These are worshippers.') and launches the campaign.

The incidents involving Gasim are a good example of the way Lean and Bolt shift emphasis, for the record of the occurrence in the Nefud in *The Seven Pillars of Wisdom:*

> . . . Gasim was my man and upon me lay the responsibility for him.
>
> I looked weakly at my trudging men, and wondered for a moment if I could change with one, sending him back on my camel to the rescue. My shirking the duty would be understood, because I was a foreigner: but that was precisely the plea I dare not set up. . .
>
> So without saying anything I turned my unwilling camel round and forced her, grunting and moaning for her camel friends, back past the long line of men, and past the baggage into the emptiness behind. My temper was very unheroic, for I was furious with my other servants, with my own play acting as a Bedouin, and most of all with Gasim . . . a

man whose engagement I regretted and of
whom I had promised to rid myself as soon as
we reached a discharging place. It seemed
absurd that I should peril my weight in the
Arab adventure for a single worthless man.

differs markedly from the movie version. When the film Lawrence is
apprised of Gasim's disappearance, he does not hestitate over going back
personally or question the 'absurdity' of the venture. Nor is his return
unnoticed:

ALI: (trying to stop Lawrence)
Gasim's time is come, Aurens. It
is written!

LAWRENCE:
Nothing is written.

ALI:
Go back then. What did you bring us here for
with your blasphemous conceit? Eh, English
blasphemer?
Akaba? What is Akaba? You shall
not be at Akaba.

   [A travelling Medium Close Shot]

LAWRENCE: (turning to answer)
I shall be at Akaba. That *is* written.   (pointing
at his head)
In here!

   [He exits.]

The disparities in the two renderings are readily apparent; but besides
subverting the book's cynicism, the adaptors use Ali, again, to clarify
their Lawrence's growing sense of, if not omnipotence, at least unim-
peachable destiny. The subsequent re-crossing of 'the sun's anvil' –
scorched earth that resembles cracked, white plaster baked to a hardness

.awrence of Arabia

vid Lean on the set of *Lawrence of Arabia.*

Above: Peter O'Toole as the legendary Thomas Edward Lawrence and Jack Hawkins as General Allenby.

Below: Peter O'Toole.

Above: Auda, brigand chief of the Howeitat (Anthony Quinn), reacts angrily when Lawrence publicly taunts him with being a servant of the Turkish overlords.

Overleaf: The Arab attack on the Turkish stronghold of Akaba.

Below: Lawrence (Peter O'Toole) acquires two new disciples – Farraj (Michel Ray) and Daud (John Dimech) kneeling before Sherif Ali (Omar Sharif). Pushing the boys is Gasim (I. S. Johar).

Lawrence of Arabia (Peter O'Toole) and his Bedouin allies blow up a Turkish troop train in the Arabian desert

which the tread of camels fails to disturb – becomes a matter of inner conviction rather than doubt, not a case of necessity (done to avoid losing face) but of willfulness. From an incident which occupies a single chapter (out of fifteen in Book Four: 'The Expedition Against Akaba'), Lean and Bolt fashion a key episode in the 'journeying' phase of *Lawrence of Arabia*. In the original, Lawrence agrees with Auda who has ridden back to rescue the rescuer: ' "For that thing, not worth a camel's price . . . " I interrupted him with, "Not worth a half-crown, Auda".' But in an epic construction, the return for Gasim cannot be 'unheroic:' it must become a display of charismatic authority, culminating with Lawrence's unassisted (and unexpected by those who presumed him dead) ride back into camp. In a tight medium close shot, he levels his penetrating gaze at Ali and uncovers his face; but before drinking he defiantly re-asserts that 'Nothing is written.' Or rather Lawrence will write; for that is the self-conscious purpose in his action, in finding the 'lost sheep,' in saving the 'dead' as ostentatiously and dramatically as Christ raised Lazarus, in demonstrating that he is more god than blasphemer.

Fatalistically (and characteristically, from Lean and Bolt's past work), Lawrence must ultimately lose in the question of 'what is written.' The execution of Gasim is original to the film, and it provides a kind of anticline to the summit of Lawrence's success in traversing the Nefud and recruiting Auda abu Tayi (postponed from an earlier position in the book). After Lawrence murders to placate the rival factions, the Harith and Howeitat chieftains exchange words on his display of emotion:

AUDA:
What ails the Englishman?

ALI:
That that he killed was the man
he brought out of the Nefud.

AUDA:
Ah, then it was written.

176

The conclusions are inevitable. Previously, Ali and Lawrence had casually discussed his 'identity,' ('Not El Aurens, just Lawrence') with Lawrence divulging his illegitimacy. For the Bedouin such a lack of heritage is tantamount to a lack of being; but Ali's recommendation ('It seems to me that you are free to choose your own name. El Aurens is best.') advances a cycle of rebirth. The contingent factor is that 'He for who nothing is written may write himself a clan.' Lawrence is legitimized: he dons Harith robes and his uniform is ritualistically burned, then he goes off to marvel at his new apparel, his new being. In medium close shot he draws his knife and stares at the blade to adjust his headgear; he laughs, spreads his arms to the wind, and watches his outstretched shadow running over the sand. In this scene, the first stage of Lawrence's 'transfiguration' is completed – his godlike portion is grasped. But before the battle, lurching away from Gasim's body, it is the demonic half that is discovered. Despite Ali's reassurances ('You gave life and you took it. The writing is still yours.'), Lawrence cannot come to grips with the full nature of 'El Aurens.' When he makes out a voucher for Auda's mercenary gold ('Signed in his Majesty's absence by. . . me.'), there is a telling pause, an uncertainty over his own name.

The Akaba sequence ends with the fall of the 'invincible' city. Lean's camera, in sweeping travelling shots, follows Lawrence's mounted Arab army as it overruns the Turkish garrison – to find, as El Aurens had predicted, that the guns were indeed fixed impotently towards the sea. After the fighting, Lawrence passes before a golden sunset at the edge of the sea. Here Lean extends his color metaphor, adding to the burning orange of the sun which seems to set fire to the water, the red of the wreath which Ali throws to the conqueror. Both characterize Lawrence's dynamism; but the wreath is also the color of blood. For as fearful as he is of killing (of the unanticipated pleasure he felt when he shot Gasim), it is too late for Lawrence to put off his heroic robes, to avert his fate. He prepares to return to Cairo to report the victory:

AUDA:
You will cross the Sinai?

177

LAWRENCE:
Why not? Moses did.

AUDA:
And will you take the children?

LAWRENCE:
Moses did.

AUDA: (shouting after him)
Moses was a prophet and beloved of God . . .

The return to Cairo traces a full circle, ending Lawrence's series of journeys and costing him another follower (Daud) in the process. It also confirms his re-baptism as El Aurens, invalidating Ali's doubts ('I see. In Cairo you will put off these funny clothes, tell stories of our ignorance and barbarity. Then they will believe you.') and ostracizing Lawrence in the officer's club from his own kind. This realization comes upon him like the ship looming up out of the dunes, hits him as tangibly as the water Farraj throws on his brooding visage, leaves him (as Allenby says) 'riding the whirlwind.'

Lawrence does not 'grow in wisdom before God,' only in confusion about his 'calling' and alienation from his fellows, first English then Bedouin. While there is little doubt that Lean and Bolt's sympathies are with Lawrence, they do remain aware of one man's limitations, of his fallibilities, and of society's repressive action against the introverted and alone. He may have visions of a 'pillar of fire,' but his corporeal being can still sink in loose sand. Accordingly, Lawrence becomes more compulsive. Feisal sums up one aspect of it to the newsman, Bentley, 'With Mr. Lawrence, mercy is a passion. With me it is merely good manners. You may judge which is the more reliable.' Whether stepping out in front of the guns to fire a flare or watching as a scalded Turkish officer empties his revolver at him, Lawrence grows fascinated with his own recklessness, tests his own legend (Auda: You are using up your nine lives. . .'

Lawrence: 'Didn't you know? They can only kill me with a golden bullet.'). When he parades atop the wrecked train, his arm and palms bloodied, framed against the sun, Lawrence still has, figuratively and literally, some self-control. But gradually it slips away from him, like the numbers of his men returning to their homes.

Lawrence's sardonic reply to Bentley's question, 'What is it that attracts you personally to the desert?' – 'It's clean' – is made bitter by the death of Farraj, for it cannot remain clean stained with the blood and littered with the bodies of his disciples. That fact is too hard to face up to: by the time Lawrence and Ali reconnoiter a Turkish-held town, he has insulated himself totally in his own myth – 'Do you think I am just anybody, Ali?' He flaunts his presence before the street patrols, arms outstretched again, exultantly walking on water (a rain puddle). Ali raises his eyes anxiously: 'Be patient with him, God.' 'Peace, Ali,' Lawrence replies, smiling, 'I am invisible.'

But he is not invisible. The pawing of the Turkish commandant and the beating – back bare, spread-eagled on a narrow bench with a grinning private holding him down – sober him, make him fearful of crucifixion. For within all the levels of allegory, the sting of the whip becomes the momentary truth, pain the proof of mortality. Discarded and groveling in the mud, he cannot dodge that realization, cannot keep terror from undermining his ill-defined inner strength, cannot avoid existing on a human level. El Aurens is arrogant, conceited, sadomasochistic, and possibly homosexual; or, as more directly stated by Auda, 'He is not perfect.' The pleasure violence and pain gave him, his unwillingness to be a subordinate, his frustrated fervor for Arab nationalism – all are human failings, and as such Lawrence admits to them with difficulty. But when he tries to back away, to retreat into this aspect of himself – 'The truth is I'm just an ordinary man' – primal elements contradict him. If the scars on his back do not quite make him a scourged Christ, his ill-fitting tan uniform (the others now wear green) mutely affirms that he is no longer just another soldier. Lawrence protests ('All right, I'm extraordinary. So what of it?'), but Allenby has an answer for

179

that also – the cup cannot pass away. In low angle medium close shot, Lawrence looks sadly skyward.

As Akaba was the Messianic confirmation, the massacre of the re-treating Turkish column is the fulfilment of the Satanic Lawrence. Rushing frenziedly amid the gunbursts and the dying, revolver smoking, curved dagger red, Lawrence shoots holes in men already dead. The signs of obsessive madness that merely seeped out, like the lines of blood traced across his back, now flare out, like the purple flag that sweeps past his face prior to the attack: and Lawrence is bound back for England (with Feisal mouthing the irony, 'El Aurens is a sword with two edges. We are equally glad to be rid of him, are we not?').

Aurens and Lawrence, the two-edged sword, merciful and murderous, framed in painful half-tone of light and dark before his betrayers, a man who could not be a god – one and both remain a paradox which Lean and Bolt choose not to unravel. There is pity for, but not penetration into this character who has descended into the maelstrom and come up mortally touched. Lawrence's dream of an Arab state ends in ignominious tribal dissension. Auda drifts off; Ali disappears into the shadows. Lawrence leaves the conference with Allenby's promise of his own cabin on a boat home. As he moves distractedly through the hotel lobby towards a waiting car, the medical officer who called him a 'filthy little wog' at the hospital (and whom Lean and Bolt will wryly select to defend Lawrence's memory at the hero's funeral) approaches him to ask a favor:

OFFICER:
I say, it's Colonel Lawrence,
isn't it?
    [Lawrence nods wearily]
Well, may I shake your hand,
sir?
    [He takes Lawrence's hand]
Just want to be able to say
I've done it, sir.

180

Lawrence walks off into his own darkness; but the officer's reactions indicate that he has failed to notice anything unusual. To him, Major T. E. Lawrence has already ceased to be. The myth has so completely concealed the man that the 'true' Lawrence is gone, apotheosized into oblivion.

He drives one last time down a desert road; a motorcycle speeds past raising dust, a shuddering omen. His eyes glance up for a moment then fall back into an effete gaze, half-obscured by a dirty windshield, as the pillar of fire is quenched.

*   *   *   *   *

The logistics involved in a motion picture like *Lawrence of Arabia* would be enough to discourage most directors: over three years of scripting, shooting, and editing; thousands of extras and miscellaneous Moroccan armies, reconstruction of sections of Damascus, Cairo, Jerusalem, and Akaba, and months of isolation in the desert where temperatures reach 130°. Still, through all of this, the end result can objectively be viewed as a textbook example of economic and direct filmmaking. The editing, from the first, is a model of precision: the prologue moves from a foreboding overhead medium shot of the motorcycle under the titles to point of view travellings as red warnings signs flash by intercut with broken sunlight coming through the trees and striking Lawrence's face and ends with a montage of his twisting body and the camera being subjectively hurled forward. Lean moves from Lawrence's precipitous death, from a close shot of the cycle's rear wheel spinning (and, co-incidentally, a fitting image for the thread of Lawrence's life), to a panning shot down the front of St. Paul's and the contentious mourners, establishing in less than five minutes an interpretive referent for the rest of the film. And every subsequent scene has a specific value in terms of narrative progression. No sunset or windstorm photographed by Freddie Young is extraneous, but functions to developed character or clarify situations. Even the battles are never gratuitously extended (a temptation with such a budget and so many

181

extras). The two principal encounters – at Akaba and with the Turkish column – are good examples of sequences helping to define the emotion of respective moments in Lawrence's life. The first with its extreme long shots and moving camera surges with the energy of Lawrence's promised 'Miracle.' The second, with its claustrophobic and smoke-filled medium close and close shots, reflects the oppressive madness of the now bloody liberator.

While *Lawrence of Arabia* is as much a character study as *Madeleine, Great Expectations, Summer Madness,* or any of the 'smaller' films, Lean does not subjectify the picture as he might have before. Perhaps that is because Lawrence, unlike Pip or Henry Hobson or even Nicholson, is less a figure to urge identification with than to take the absolute measure of, one whose stature *is* genuinely larger than life and whose feelings can be externalized only to a limited degree. As with Ridgefield and *The Sound Barrier,* the very core of *Lawrence of Arabia* is the lingering inscrutability of a hero with a vision, of one, again, who cannot be fully empathized with, who must live as he dreams – alone.

Chapter 10

DOCTOR ZHIVAGO (1965)

And what if all animated nature
Be but organic Harps diversely fram'd,
That tremble into thought, as o'er them sweeps
Plastic and vast, one intellectual breeze,
At once the Soul of each, and God of all?

Samuel Coleridge, 'The Eolian Harp'

AFTER THE EMOTIONALLY and physically exhausting experience of *Lawrence,* Lean returned to the eternal triangle with an adaptation of Boris Pasternak's *Doctor Zhivago.* This new project provided several immediate challenges. The first was its sprawling narrative line, spanning over four decades of Czarist/Soviet history and, in the process, introducing multifarious characters in the tradition of the great Russian novels. Like *The Brothers Karamzov* or *War and Peace,* the very bulk of *Doctor Zhivago* defied any attempt at rigorously 'faithful' condensation for the screen, even in a format of approximately three hours running time (the producer's original aim). Lean and Bolt realized at the start that the book's intricate interplay of human characters against the socially complex panorama of world war and revolution could not be capsulized

183

without doing serious damage to the characters themselves and the concepts they represented, without resulting in sketchiness or confusion. Accordingly, they worked to circumvent an equally strong tradition (as upheld by King Vidor's *War And Peace* or Richard Brooks' *The Brothers Karamazov*) of failure in bringing the 'epic' Russian novel to the screen.

'Time [in Pasternak's novel] is not covered flowingly but in sudden leaps. At the end of Chapter 14 Lara and Yuri have parted, Strelnikov has shot himself; the main story is over. Chapter 15 commences, "It remains to tell the brief story of the last eight or ten years of Yuri's life . . . " and finishes with the reported death of Lara. At the start of Chapter 16 another gulf of years has been jumped; we learn of the existence of Yuri and Lara's daughter, now grown-up, and hear from her the story of her childhood . . . As if this were not enough, the last section of this chapter begins, "Five or ten years later . . ." ' Because of these problems described by Bolt, much of the novel's final section was excised and, instead, the triangle (consisting of Zhivago, his wife Tonya, and his mistress Lara) was stressed.

Even with this bit of editing, the final screenplay and subsequent film betray certain inadequacies. Lean has said that the history and revolution of the film 'simply provide the canvas against which is told a moving and highly personal story.' In his *Lawrence of Arabia* and *Ryan's Daughter* this is indeed the case: he effectively stylizes and simplifies the historical elements so that the more personal moments of the story may develop unobstructed. But unfortunately *Zhivago* suffers from an overdose of simplistic history and social drama. The factions of the revolutionary struggle in Russia are populated by caricatures. The Czarists are exploitive, hedonistic, and arrogant (from Komarovsky to the Dragoon Colonel who is pommeled to death by the retreating army). The Bolsheviks such as Comrade Yelkin, Razin, and to a lesser degree Zhivago's own half-brother are joyless, ruthless, and unrecalcitrant. These characters are never treated with distinction; yet they occupy a good deal of screen time. They are merely convenient stereotypes of the opposing sides; and this tendency overlaps into some of the major figures. A good example of a potentially tragic but underdeveloped characterization is Pasha. This disappointed idealist begins as a naive radical, as an organizer of workers' rallies who loves Lara for her assumed innocence. Ultimately, he is disappointed in both and seeks to bury his emotions beneath a new persona – General Strelnikov, the merciless demagogue ('The private life is dead'). His story is a gripping one, but, as Lara and Yuri demand most of the screen time, it must remain peripheral. Eventually Pasha is dropped completely, and his suicidal end is merely reported by Komarovsky. Lean and Bolt, having restructured the original, were still not bold enough in their cuts. Characters such as this one either had to be expanded and explicated (which meant a longer film) or dropped altogether.

But for all its problems, *Zhivago*'s central concern is well-focused. The essential movement of all of Lean's motion pictures, no matter how deeply enmeshed in history, might be termed 'anti-social.' This does not mean that Lean is unconcerned with social issues (his choice of subjects, if anything, implies the opposite); but it should be clear by now that his sympathies fall to the individual, to his plight during moments of social crisis or his conflct with social convention. Yuri Zhivago, the poet-doctor, is a fitting Lean hero. Imbued with a strong desire for life (Strelnikov: 'And what will you do, with your wife and child, in Varykino?' Zhivago: 'Just live.'), he sees beauty in even the ugliest moments (in the stomach-pumping of Lara's mother for example); and his poetry is extremely personal and introspective ('Petit-bourgeois and self-indulgent,' say the revolutionaries). Although he can sympathize with the revolution, he places personal creation and individual worth on a higher scale of values.

'The madding crowd' in Lean's work is always a fickle and frequently repressive conception. In *Oliver Twist, Madeleine,* and *Ryan's Daughter* crowds violently obstruct the respective hero and heroines (Oliver's capture after the theft of Brownlow's handkerchief Madeleine's ride to the courthouse; Rosy's punishment) or, as the winds change course, take the main character's part (the Londoners rescuing Oliver from Sikes; the crowd cheering Madeleine after the Trial; Rosy's earlier wedding reception). In *Doctor Zhivago* the representation of this concept is fairly direct. More often than not, Lara and Yuri are moving against the flow of history. Among Czarists and bourgeoisie, Yuri is a proponent of the workers' cause; yet when the revolution does finally come, he has misgivings about the style of life advocated by the Bolsheviks. Contrary to their advice, he continues to compose his 'absurdly personal' (Strelnikov's denotation) poetry. Further the revolution and its revolutionaries, like the war and its warriors, become less socially beneficent and more personally disruptive factors. In the end, Yuri's own death (by heart attack) is indirectly brought on by the crowd of passengers in a streetcar preventing him from reaching a girl he believes is Lara.

This emphasis on the personal, on *amour fou,** is most intensely felt and idealized at Varykino, with Lara. The setting seems, at first glance, transposed from some medieval romance. The summer mansion topped by frosted Byzantine cupolas and covered inside and out with artificial snow and cellophane resembles a fairy-tale ice castle. As Lara and Yuri open the door, the chandelier tinkles and a breeze softly stirs and drifts. The couple wanders in hesitantly, in wonderment: in this other-worldly atmosphere their hope of one 'last mad idyl' [Bolt's description] resides. Here, too, Yuri is able to write again, sitting at a table in the sunroom which is stocked almost miraculously with blank paper, a new pen, and a full inkwell. As the wolves – symbols of a hostile outer world slowly closing in – howl outside, the balalaika sounds defiantly on the track. In this magical place, as Yuri fashions his 'Lara cycle' of sonnets over her demurral ('This isn't me, Yuri.' It's you.'), the act of artistic creation is given a mystical aura.

> O wild West Wind, thou breath of
> Autumn's being,
> Thou, from those unseen presence
> the leaves dead

* Defined by Luis Bunuel as 'Love [which] isolates the lovers, makes them indifferent to all the social conventions or familial obligations, leads them to destruction. A love which astonishes . . .'

Doctor Zhivago

ri Zhivago (Omar Sharif) and Tonya Gromeko (Geraldine Chaplin) in *Doctor Zhivago*.

above: The framing for the flashback: In an attempt to draw out recognition in The Girl's – Tonya's (Rita Tushingham) – face, General Zhivago (Alec Guinness) – believing she is the lost child born to the poet doctor and Lara – shows her the book of Zhivago's poetry.

left: The frightened but still courageous group Zhivago (Omar Sharif), Lara and her child (Julie Christie and Lucy Westmore) await the inevitable return of Komarovsky to the Varykino house.

right: Lara (Julie Christie) is shocked at Pasha's (Tom Courtenay') slashed face received during a Moscow street demonstration.

t: Mounted Dragoons ride down the demonstrators during their march through the Moscow streets in
05.

ow: Determined to seek revenge on her seducer and tormenter Komarovsky, Lara (Julie Christie) in
ctor Zhivago raises her gun to kill him amid the festivities of the Sventytski Christmas Party.

Below: Russian soldiers battle against nature as well as German opposition in the biting winter cold.

Right: Russian partisans prepa to ride to their winter encampment.

Director David Lean warms himself and contemplates between scenes on a wintry location site of *Doctor Zhivago* near Soria in northern Spain.

Are driven, like ghosts from an
enchanter fleeing.

[Percy Bysshe Shelley]

For the Romantic poets the emotional and metaphysical was the soul of the artist and his artistry. This concept does not appear, in any significant way, in Pasternak's *Zhivago,* but it does in the film. The flashbacks which frame the entire story (and which are also original to the film) begin with the funeral of Yuri's mother – a 'simple woman' who had a talent for the balalaika. The birth-death cycle is played to its fullest expression here: after a shot of the mother entombed in her casket, Lean cuts to a rush of wind blowing the leaves about Yuri and the strains of his mother's 'enchanting' balalaika are heard (sounding like the film's Eolian harp). With visual and aural correlatives to Shelley's ode, the gift of inspiration has been passed. Yuri, like his mother, will become an artist. The physical symbol of this gift, the balalaika, is left to Yuri; and Yuri in turn will give it to his and Lara's daughter. This becomes the closing note in the final scene, as Zhivago's half-brother tries to convince a young girl (Tonya) that she is Yuri and Lara's child:

> GENERAL ZHIVAGO:
> Tonya!
> [Tonya and her companion turn towards him].
> Can you play the balalaika?
>
> THE YOUNG ENGINEER:
> Can she play . . .
>
> GENERAL ZHIVAGO:
> She plays well?
>
> YOUNG ENGINEER: (nudging Tonya who
> does not answer)
> She's an artist!
>
> GENERAL ZHIVAGO:
> An artist . . . Who taught you?

YOUNG ENGINEER:
No one taught her.

GENERAL ZHIVAGO:
Ah. Then it's a gift.

The last shots are of water pouring through a dam, resuming its natural course. The continuity of life, natural forces, and artistic inspiration overcome the man-made obstructions (cf. the dam in *Brief Encounter*).

The whole scheme of nature analogies and color is systematically worked out in *Doctor Zhivago.* White has a prominent position; basically it can connote purity and innocence, as with Mary Justin in *The Passionate Friends* or Jane Hudson in *Summer Madness,* and with Tonya Gromeko in *Zhivago.* The idyl at Varykino like the one spent in the Alps by the lovers of *Passionate Friends* develops images of isolation and insulation. In escaping the same social structures, Lara and Yuri retreat to their fortress of 'silent, secret snow;'' but only until the sun melts the protective layers and leaves them exposed.

In this film, the 'life-force' is primarily associated with Lara, through her symbols and her colors. Yellow is hers – the sunflowers with which she decorates the hospital and her rooms at Yuriatin, the dissolve from a daffodil to her face, even the sun which Zhivago follows through the forest near Yuriatin. When Lara leaves the army hospital, Lean uses this symbol for a psychological exposition in a cut from her wilting sunflowers to a dejected Yuri, walking past. Further, the first physical contact of the lovers, on a streetcar, is undercut with sparks from its electric power cable. For Lara is an electric, catalytic force in Zhivago's existence, the inspiring energy which the life-seeking poet needs to create.

The forces of nature also inspire Zhivago. To escape the city, Yuri and his family ride in a crowded cattle car: at every opportunity during the journey, Zhivago slides open a slat and stares out at the countryside. The moon is what he concentrates on as he peers from the train; the moon is what he follows when he deserts the Red Guards and returns to Lara. By then it has become more than a Keatsian ideal of 'high romance,' become

196

a white, symbolic 'power' linking nature with life (Lara) and re-animating it.*

For one of the few times in his films, Lean also deals with a degradation of the life-force. The person who introduces Lara to the world of sensuality is Komarovsky, the venal government official. His color is red (the decor of his house, the walls of the restaurant where he takes Lara, the dress he purchases for her). However, as vulgar and corrupt as he is, he fanatically devotes himself to living (to those 'not high-minded, not pure, but *alive*') and acts as the prime mover in Lara's recognition of her own desires and needs.

Lean's direct, dialectical cutting style re-inforces these images without superseding them. The cut from Lara and Yuri accidentally touching to a spark on the cables is clearly part of an associational montage but also acts as a subjectification of sensation *and* a dynamic metaphor anticipating Lara's future relation to Zhivago. In the series of cuts after her 'rape' by Komarovsky (Lara's tear-stained face; a gun; Lara at Komarovsky's door), Lean subjectively accelerates (in the context of Lara's distraction) and summarizes visually what could have deteriorated into dull exposition. One of the most noted sequences of the film, the massacre of the protestors (a mutation of the 'Odessa Steps' in *Battleship Potemkin*), is an extension of the hanging scene in *Great Expectations*, wherein Lean shifts the emphasis from the horrifying event to the reactions of one individual (in this instance, Zhivago) – a shift from the 'objective reality' and structural awareness of Eisenstein to the 'subjective' and personal cons-ciousness of Lean, exemplifying the difference between a populist and an individualist.

*　　*　　*　　*　　*

Maurice Jarre scorred all three of Lean's latest pictures. His expressive combination of selective atonality and rich melodiousness follows in the

---

* A conceit established by Dante Gabriel Rossetti in 'A Match with the Moon:' 'Weary already, weary miles to-night/I walked for bed: and so, to get some ease,/ I dogged the flying moon with similes./

And like a wisp she doubled on my sight/ In ponds; and caught in tree-tops like a kite;/ And in a globe of film all vapourish/ Swam full-faced like a silly silver fish.'

traditions of the music of Lean's earlier films. The technique favored most with Jarre is the crescendo-diminuendo: in *Zhivago* it occurs most strikingly after a scene of love between Lara and Yuri followed by a travelling in to Yuri and Tonya's cottage at Varykino. The crescendo balalaika overlaps from the prior scene, but as the camera enters the house and frames Yuri lying guiltily by his wife's side, the music becomes atonal and diminishes abruptly. A similar juxtaposition of image and sound is employed in *Ryan's Daughter* when Shaughnessy awakens to discover Rosy and her lover locked in an embrace outside; in *Lawrence Of Arabia*, as the camera sweeps in to a vista of Auda's camp; and in *Bridge On The River Kwai*, moving from a victorious Colonel Nicholson being paraded on the shoulders of his men to the sobs of a beaten Saito.

Chapter 11

RYAN'S DAUGHTER (1970)

Dance there upon the shore;
What need have you to care
For wind or water's roar?
What need have you to dread
The monstrous crying of the wind?

> *W. B. Yeats, 'To a Child*
> *Dancing in the Wind'*

It was at present a place perfectly accordant
with man's nature – neither ghastly, hateful,
not ugly: neither common-place, unmeaning, nor
tame; but, like a man, slighted and enduring;
and withal singularly colossal and mysterious . . .
It had a lonely face, suggesting tragical possibilities.

> *Thomas Hardy,* The Return
> of the Native

BLACK CLOUDS AND red-tinged mists fly from the face of the sun, as if an
empyreal journey through open space were beginning. Gradually gliding

back from this dark, preternatural world, green hillocks rolling past are revealed. A sea-wind swirls up the cliffside, and Rosy Ryan perched on its edge helplessly watches her lost parasol fall to the waves. But father Hugh, fisher of flotsam and men – and not apt to distinguish between the two – fetches it back as he shakes the salt water from his billowing cassock. Little enough, it seems, to begin with.

It seems; for Rosy Ryan, like Laura Jesson or Mary Justin, like Madeleine or Jane, is another discontented, idle dreamer ('What do you do with yourself, Rose?'). She reads, but hers is the fictional fiction (*The King's Mistress* by Raoul du Barry) of youth; and at every opportunity she leaves the browns and drab greens of her village for the rougher symmetry of the coast, for the fragrant wild heather and the glistening blue and emerald of the sea with its sharp spray. This day, it is to meet Charles Shaughnessy, the schoolmaster who taught her about 'Byron and Beethoven and Captain Blood,' and in whose footsteps (despite his caution that 'I'm not one of those fellers myself') she would gladly walk, literally and figuratively. But even as close-ups catch her bare foot slipping into the imprint of his boot and her smile at this small accomplishment, Lean cuts back to an extra long shot: the relentless tide surges in all around, nearly throwing her off balance and erasing the tracks. With deceptive ease, Lean brings these familiar elements into play. The conflict of the fanciful and the everyday, the pantheistic forces of wind and sea, empathy for a young girl given over to Romantic yearnings – all are contained in these first few minutes of film. Subsequently, as the dull 'realities' of Rosy's situation – her ordinary, slightly tattered clothes; the coarse, meager abodes of the inhabitants of Kirrary; the sluttish manner of the village girls; even the craggy, sunbaked visage of the local priest – are detailed, her desire for escape and adventure become more understandable. A tension is immediately introduced between the pristine 'villageness' of Kirrary and Ryan's pub with its smoke-filled, common-house atmosphere and the isolated sea beach and woodlands, between conflicting spheres of influence which are, again, essentially artificial and natural.

On a thematic level, Lean and screenwriter Bolt remain fairly explicit. 'You were meant for the wide world, Rose,' Charles tells her; and as Rosy widens her search after life, after what Bolt calls 'intenser modes of feeling,' she strays closer to that 'monstrous wind' which threatens more than her parasol.* But then the sun is what she seeks. She marries Charles only to discover that he is no more than what he warned ('You've mistaken a penny mirror for the sun'), that wedlock is as unelectric as Father Hugh had speculated:

> FATHER COLLINS: (reading)
> Now 'Marriage is a sacrament ordained by
> God . . ' That means, Rosy, that once it's done,
> it isn't up to me; nor you; nor Charles; it's
> done; till one or the other of you is dead.
>
> ROSY:
> I understand that, Father.
>
> FATHER COLLINS:
> Mp. Now God ordained it for three reasons.
> First, that you an' Charles should be a comfort
> to each other – in the long, dull days an'
> weary evenin's. You understand that?
>
> ROSY:
> Yes.
>
> FATHER COLLINS:
> Mp. Well, second for the procreation of good
> children an' to bring 'em up good Catholics.
> D'you understand that?
>
> ROSY:
> Yes.

* Hawthorne describes an urge akin to Rosy's in, aptly enough, 'Footprints on the Seashore:' 'At intervals and not infrequent ones, the forests and the ocean summon me – one with the roar of its waves, the other with the murmur of its boughs – forth from the haunts of men.'

FATHER COLLINS:
And thirdly: for the satisfaction of the flesh.

ROSY: (quickly)
– Yes.

FATHER COLLINS: (gently)
Are you scared of that?

ROSY:
Yes.

FATHER COLLINS:
It's nothing to be scared of, Rosy. A function of the body.

ROSY:
I suppose all girls is a bit scared, before.

FATHER COLLINS:
All fellers, too.

ROSY:
Yes?

FATHER COLLINS:
Oh, yes.

ROSY: (quietly)
It'll make me a different person . . . won't it?

FATHER COLLINS:
Marriage?

ROSY:
The . . . satisfaction of the flesh.

FATHER COLLINS:
Well, it's a gate I've not been through myself.
            (Reassuring; amused)
No, it won't make you a different person.

ROSY:

I want it to.

FATHER COLLINS:

Child, what're you expectin'?

> [She struggles for an answer. She searches
> the sky. Father Hugh's gaze follows hers. He
> sees a gull against the sky.]

FATHER COLLINS:

Wings is it?

After her marriage, still unpinioned, Rosy flees down the beach, disillusioned, despondent, and tearful, only to encounter the grizzled old cleric. He offers nothing but rebuke. He tells her that there are no wings, that (as Yeats puts it) 'girls at puberty may find, the first Adam in their thought' does not fulfil their flesh. 'There must be something more, Father Hugh,' she argues. 'Why – Glory to God – Why must there be? Because Rosy Ryan wants it?' He answers her defiant 'Aye!' with a slap, like a crusty bishop simultaneously confirming her adulthood and admonishing against sinful wishes: 'You can't help having 'em [wishes], but don't nurse 'em or sure to God you'll get what you're wishing!'

At this dramatically central point, there is a dissolve to a bus stopping at a lonely country crossroads. Someone gets off. As the bus rattles on its way, the shadowy figure of a tall, young man dressed in a British Army uniform is revealed. A vehicle arrives to meet him, and – as he slowly moves to board it – a close shot of his polished boots emphasizes a physical impendiment: he limps, rather markedly. Major Doryan arrives like a hobbled Apollo gone to earth in a burned-out chariot, arrives to answer Rosy's yearning in a flurry of sensual rapture, to sweep her up into a transcendent passion, set as Romantic love 'should' be (as Laura Jesson might have envisioned it from her train compartment) against ruined medieval towers, in sea caves and sheltered groves. Significantly, Doryan does not first encounter Rosy in such transistory settings as a tea room or sidewalk cafe or streetcar, but in the familiar (to her) front room

203

of her father's tavern. Their second meeting takes place behind her husband's schoolhouse. Doryan swiftly becomes a fixture in Rosy's everyday life. The end result is that – unlike Laura or Mary Justin or Jane – Rosy does not have control over the affair; she has no place to run away or back to. Part of the reason for this is that Doryan is not just another English officer back from the front but very much a 'creation' of the heroine, someone conjured up as Emile L'Angelier was by Madeleine in a moment of wishful thinking – a notion re-inforced directly by the dissolve from such a thought to Doryan's arrival and indirectly by his entry into the pub while Rosy reads a book of poems as if sprung from the pages of verse. Doryan intrudes powerfully, almost metaphysically, and Lean exploits this intrusion (much as he did in the first shot of L'Angelier and, again, unlike *Brief Encounter, Summer Madness* or *Doctor Zhivago*) to interpolate boldly the usual progression from initial acquaintance to love (takes advantage, in a sense, of audience anticipation) and literally throws Rosy and Doryan together.

Figurative Usage. Andrew Doryan is not the 'perfect' Byronic hero, not tailored to the imagination of his heroine as closely as L'Angelier was, but rather a genuinely imperfect one: sullen, vulnerable, too mysterious to penetrate, even limping as Byron himself did. If anyone, Doryan most resembles Lawrence of Arabia, in his very appearance and manner, in his introspective attitude, even in his fixed, compulsive stares. As with Lawrence, Lean expresses Doryan's character through physical detail and associational imagery. His mien, from the spotlessness of his boots which conceal his deformity to the sallowness of his clean-shaven face even to the methodical manner in which he taps cigarettes against his silver case, suggests a suppressed but lingering disquiet – all conveyed so strongly that when he flashes back to the trenches and a black shell burst fills the screen, it clearly reflects the explosive state of his own afflicted mind. More of Doryan's character is clarified by the basic but pliable arrangement of his figure in a landscape. He stands, at first glance, leaning slightly, eyes fixed directly ahead, and behind him the dusky strip of sky that separates the brown earth from the blue-black clouds stretches narrowly. A close shot frames his head against this oppressive overcast as he peers – his face lit in a gray half-tone (exactly as Lawrence's was in his last meeting with Allenby) rendered almost impressionistically, as if reflected from the ground below him – down painfully at his sole welcomer, Michael, the crippled village fool. Later, in his rendezvous with Rosy, his figure hurrying awkwardly across the skyline in silhouette will alternate with high angle medium shots where he sits in his room, confined and motionless in the semi-darkness.

Charles Shaughnessy's figure, in contrast, avoids the skyline. He is framed instead against the solid (though) stained walls of his schoolhouse or the flat-painted green door of his parlor In the beach scene where Charles discovers the footprints of Rosy and Doryan leading towards a tidal cave, he falls back from the realization (*from* the footprints on the right side of the frame) against a massive gray rock. When he leaves Rosy in the middle of the night, he wanders towards a shelf in the cliff by an inlet and there sits among large gray stones. Against this background, he is as solid and permanent as Doryan is temporary and illusive (physically and in Rosy's life), finds support in the terrain which seems so visually hostile to Doryan.

The use of color is perhaps most clearly defined in terms of Rosy. Her garb when walking down the beach to meet Charles is fairly prosy: beige and dark gray (like the rocks), a straw hat with paper flowers, neat but threadbare, a drab costume at best, which she feebly tries to improve with a pendant watch and incongruous lace gloves. Even her parasol (purchased at auction by her father from a dead woman's possessions) for all its frilliness is a simple, unstartling black and white. Later, the prospects for her marriage are summed up in the colorations of two point-of-view shots as she lies in bed waiting for Charles: a stained brown ceiling and a window (as in *Madeleine* both a sexual symbol and an opening to a less restricted world) glowing red, representations of the spoiled everyday and the unusually bright, of the dismal and the ecstatic. What she gets are the stained walls of Charles' schoolhouse, the same walls the camera panned across slowly while she waited for him to emerge from his parlor and propose to her. The only deep (the only strongly felt) color which is ever added to that parlor is the tiny fringe of red cloth which Rosy will later fix beneath a white plaster bust of Beethoven. Rosy contents herself with wearing beige and gray, but parts of the decor begin to embody her spirit, such as the tarnished brass bedposts and the door to the bedroom which she paints a bright yellow and against which she is repeatedly framed. (In her return home after riding with Doryan, Rosy retreats to that bedroom behind that yellow door. Lean frames Charles standing against his green door in medium shot behind her close-up, so that he is 'held' at a distance from her between her door and the sill).

It isn't until her meeting with Doryan in the pub that Rosy's color begins to blaze: a bright yellow spot reflects in the mirror behind her; as she serves him, a close shot catches yellow liquid swirling in a glass; and, after Doryan's seizure has passed and the lights have come up again, the brownish wall behind them seem suddenly suffused with yellow. As the love affair intensifies, she even takes his colors: the red petticoat (which Doryan saw hanging on the line as he rode past the school on the day of his arrival) and black shawl she wears to go riding are his, those of his dress uniform. In Charles' fantasy of her and Doryan strolling like young lovers on the beach, she will wear a yellow dress (but only in fantasy is it possible for she doesn't own a yellow dress – another figurative mark of the affair's impermanence). And when the two storms, of the sea and of her passion, have abated, Charles' words ('I'm going to leave you, Rose.') will drain the color from the door behind her, as a final trope for her position.

Archetypal Imagery; Pantheism. Lean and Bolt also develop a more primordial system of relationships in *Ryan's Daughter*. As were Lara and to a lesser extent Nancy and Jane Hudson, Rose is ascribed, through repeated visual links and through color, the delicate traits of her namesake. The 'wrong' Charles speaks of when he tries to convince Rosy that he is not for her is that in taking their relation beyond that of pupil and teacher, beyond the sexual segregation of the schoolroom (which even has separate entrances for boys and girls) into the parlor and the bedroom, he is compelled literally to 'deflower' her. Conscious of this, feeling guilty over it, Charles can no longer consider her a child but is incapable of responding to all her needs as a woman. Rather, he idealizes her against her wishes ('You're a wonderful girl, Rose.' 'No! No, I'm not.'); he continues to treat her like the floral specimens which he gathers, presses between the pages of an atlas, mounts, and labels.

Rosy is also like the birds whose wings she envies. Like a gull she hovers over the sea and, rock-bred, follows Charles – as Father Collins' flock follow their faith, for want of any other mysteries. Accordingly, Charles' original image as teacher begins to assume wider, Messianic dimensions. Like Magdelene Rosy walks in his footsteps; she becomes a disciple, the only one among the villagers who appreciates his tolerance (towards the British), his self-effacement, and his aesthetic insulation. Charles himself is eventually 'stigmatized' as the rough boots of the village men bloody his outstretched hands during Rosy's ordeal, fulfilling her conception of him as a long-suffering, 'rare man;' he will even wear a flowing robe and be seen walking by the water's edge.

But it is Doryan's character, of the three, that is the most completely constructed from archetype and the most enigmatic. From the first shot of him and the revelation of his agonized expression, Doryan is marked as one possessed of and by hellfire. Psychologically (realistically) he is shell-shocked; but the traits of his illness are Satanic, from the fits of shaking and his injury ('Pegleg!') to his dusky uniform and his black horse (one is tempted to say 'fiery'). His stare can wither, as it does the taunting Moureen; his disturbed (and disturbing) presence sends Michael fleeing from the room in terror. To Rosy, Doryan is not just another penny mirror, not just someone who sensually ignites her, but the sun she has been seeking all along – an identification which was previously made with Lawrence and which Lean graphically supports here in a medium close shot of Doryan seen through the windshield of a lorry and seated so that the sun is reflected squarely over his face. Later, in Michael's eyes, Doryan will even wield thunder, when he throws a detonator cap against an old boiler. He is driven by a primitive energy, surging up like the sputtering generator and driving his unearthly silhouette out across the countryside. In a sense, when Doryan arrives at Kirrary, he has already perished, mentally and physically – adding irony to the former post-commander's off-hand observation: 'You look about finished, sir.' Doryan is about finished – an 'alien' waiting in a strange place for bodily death.

Because of this vague state of being, Doryan shuns the company of his wife as he would familiar places and things. The black-and-white snapshots which the corporal unpacks and puts by his bed are of her and of a group of riders by a towered manor. So he rides with Rosy to a dark tower and for a few moments is 'normal' again. With her he can escape into a primeval world which is simpler, more passionate, and blacker in the deep shade where the moss grows on fallen trees. But even as he lies serene and sequestered in her arms, the sound of machine guns comes up on the soundtrack like a sigh, and he trembles again.

As in past films, Lean incorporates the wind and land and sea (air, earth, and water to match the human fire) into his pantheistic conception. Like the wind which skims over the cobblestones in *Madeleine* or introduces *Hobson's Choice,* Lean may use a sudden gust to snatch at Rosy's parasol or hat or, more seriously, summon a colder current that seems to cut at the viscera to frighten her on the footpath and send her scurrying back inside to Charles after a clandestine moment with Doryan. The same sort of wind moans and whistles through the trees in the glade, threatens to tear apart and destroy Rosy, the flower, as surely as Charles crushes her. It is also the demonic variant which haunts Doryan, which will neither die down nor dispel the black shadow (the black clouds, the black phantasms of shells exploding) over his soul.

Lean's use of the rugged terrain of Western Ireland is reminiscent of the moors of Emily Bronte or Thomas Hardy. Indeed, Lean is no stranger to that Hardy country 'suggesting tragical possibilities.' Both men consistently place their heroines, major and minor, in such environments:

yan's Daughter

id Lean and screenwriter Robert Bolt on the set of *Ryan's Daughter.*

Above: Charles Shaughnessy (Robert Mitchum) and Rosy Ryan (Sarah Miles) are married.

Below: Rosy (Sarah Miles) and Doryan (Christopher Jones) ride into a secluded part of the woods, enfolded by birches and carpeted with bluebells, where they make love for the first time.

ove: The lovers Rosy (Sarah Miles) and Major Doryan (Christopher Jones) in Charles' (Robert Mitchum) *tasy.*

low: The British Major Andrew Doryan (Christopher Jones) and his troops block the path of a truck *rrying* German arms to aid the Irish partisans.

To the villagers of Kirrary, Michael (John Mills, *right*) is less deserving of compassion than the lobster he holds. Father Collins (Trevor Howard) is the one man who has bothered to befriend the pathetic mute.

the prologue to *Oliver Twist,* for example, as Oliver's mother struggles across a hostile landscape to the workhouse to give birth, strongly recalls a similar effort made by Fanny in *Far from the Madding Crowd.* Bathsheba, entranced by the Byronic Troy in this novel; Tess of the D'Urbervilles; or Eustacia Vye, longing for Paris in *The Return of the Native,* are all markedly related to Rosy Ryan – whether in their innocent beauty, their willfulness, or their desire for something more than the bleak surroundings offer. Hardy's moody 'Wessex' is particularly like Kirrary in *Ryan's Daughter* – both populated by a society that reflects a natural harshness, simple traditionalism, and intolerance of independent thought or action.

Perhaps the most telling comparison between Hardy and Lean is their fatalism in regarding attempts to break from these confines or conventions. Tess ends her wanderings in illness; Eustacia in death. Bathsheba after experiencing passion with Sergeant Troy resigns herself to the solidity of Gabriel Oak – character names for which Rosy, Major Doryan, and Charles Shaughnessy could easily be substituted. In much the same way, Hardy's description of Eustacia Vye – whose 'high gods were William the Conqueror, Stratford, and Napolean Buonaparte,' whose 'instincts [were] towards social non-conformity,' and who 'seemed to long for the abstraction called passionate love more than for any particular lover' – closely parallels the state of mind which Father Hugh reports to Tom Ryan as, 'Your "princess" has fellers enough (indicating his temple) ... in here!'

Father Hugh's appraisal of Rosy is, however, considerably more generous than his opinion of the village populace: 'Devil take me if the whole lot of you is not possessed and dammed!' Short of that, Kirrary itself is still not a very typical place. Little is specified about it, its history, its industry, its prejudices other than an abiding hatred of all things British. The young men and women seem to have nothing to do besides loiter in the high street (the only street), leering and giggling, taunting Michael and incurring the pastor's anger. At times, the villagers act as just another fixture in the background, adding relief or working up to a collective frenzy at the wedding party, which Lean intercuts with Charles and Rosy upstairs as he did the highland dancers and the couple in *Madeleine.* But that group also anticipates the hostile gathering outside the school, the same faces (perhaps, for many, even the same expressions) are transformed into the kind of crowd that was a component of social repression in *Doctor Zhivago.* Throughout, the townspeople seem to be moving closer to Father Hugh's promise of perdition. Their one act of collective redemption – aiding O'Leary and the rebels – might offset the others, but for their obstinate, unregenerate ostracism of Rosy at the end. It could not be said that the villagers are evil – they lack sufficient dimension for that qualitative a judgment to be passed (as do the English soldiers, as does the constable whom O'Leary executes on the road). Nor is Kirrary merely a representation of the traits of society in general – unlike the cities of the Victorian films, it is too remote, too cut off from general society for that. Rather it becomes, mainly, another outcropping of an already animated universe and another catalyst in Rosy's existence.

The storm sequence spans and opposes all these divergent natural forces. Its overtones range from the simple sight of the ammo boxes pitching like coffins in the surf to the vaster implications of the contest of sea and land, of proverbial irresistible force and immovable object. It 'clears' the air not just in the sky but around Doryan, Rosy, and Charles, bringing secrets to the surface as it does. It is also a manifestation of some great, fateful cycle, confirming and sustaining the sense of something impending which begins with Father Hugh's remark on the clouding sky: 'You'd think they was announcing the coming of Christ.'

If the storm, with its feathery fingers of trailing mist or its crashing fistlike sheets, is the most ostensible, preternatural intervention of the hand of God, there are subtler traces of such workings throughout the film. Doryan, for example, could easily fill a kind of re-incarnative role. There are only three rifle shots fired in *Ryan's Daughter:* two when Tim O'Leary kills the constable who has recognized him; one when Doryan shoots O'Leary. In a sequence where unseen crows caw ominously over shot, the constable's body is thrown into a deep pit, yawning like the mouth of hell itself and coughing up a cloud of dust. Doryan's arrival shortly after this is never really seen. The bus pulls away and he is standing there, but he might as well have sprung from the ground (like Lawrence before Feisal or Magwitch to grab Pip) or from that black pit (as in the sequence of events in *The Sound Barrier* where the smouldering crater from Tony's crash cedes to the birth of his son). Inexorably, he is led to avenge the policeman's death (and, in part, his own tropistic 'death'). When he shoots O'Leary, in the leg (as he was shot at the front), crippling him, it is as if he had been dispatched to do so, almost – and this seems particularly true in light of his uncontrollable seizure immediately after the act – as if he were brought to it by some overwhelming elemental drive.

It is Michael who appears to be most harmoniously in accord with these forces, who, even garlanded with flowers in a grotesque parody of a grinning satyr, is most genuinely a child of nature. It is Michael, finally, who provides the means (albeit inadvertently) for Doryan's death. It is Michael who, by mimicking Doryan in the village, makes possible the understanding which precipitates violence against Rosy and who physically (by his very presence) and spiritually (by this promulgation of guilt) compels Doryan's last, inward look at himself among the skeletal ribs of a beached ship in the red glow of the setting sun. Ultimately Doryan perishes in his *own* inferno. But it is to Michael that he passes some measure of his spirit (Michael is the first and last to see him and limps after him like a shadow a few moments before he dies; afterwards there is a low angle shot of Michael leaping over a rise while Doryan's music surges in the background), as surely as he passes on his cigarette case – a 'fact' which Rosy partially senses in the final scene where she kisses Michael good-bye. With Doryan's extinction, blown back to atoms (as he sits, almost in visual pun, by a rusty old boiler or furnace), the final element – fire – merges figuratively back into the other three. He waits for the sun to go and disappears with it. And like the match striking, which flares on the track when he first comes and which flashes in the screen darkness just before his suicide – each of which foreshadows aurally the distant explosion that announces the cataclysmic release of his soul – Doryan expires in a flame, in 'flames begotten of flame, where the blood-begotten spirits come and all complexities of fury leave, dying into a dance, an agony of trance, an agony of flame . . . '(Yeats)

Subjectivity; Irony. Ryan's Daughter clearly belongs more to the title character than any other; but, as with *The Sound Barrier* or *Hobson's Choice,* Lean has a number of major figures (and, in the revolutionary sub-plot, a large section of narrative which Rosy cannot be part of) to deal with and subsequently is unable to develop the picture wholly from her viewpoint. Instead, he effectively distributes the incidents of subjective perception, fixing momentarily on the person (or persons) most appropriate. The discussion between Charles and Rosy in the schoolhouse, for instance, operates within a kind of dual point-of-view refined from the scene of Pip and Estella on the stairs in *Great Expectations.* In the early stages, a slight high angle over Charles' shoulder in the medium and medium close two shots causes him to tower over Rosy. This visually approximates both her initial disadvantage in the argument and the very conception she is consciously fighting against in the dialogue: 'I feel like a child in this place – and I'm not a child, d'you know that?' The music on the track (a record of Beethoven's Fifth Symphony playing in the parlor) 'belongs' to Charles in that he admires and has chosen to play it; but it gives voice equally to Rosy's idealized notions of Charles, to *her* misguided perception of him as a noble or heroic Romantic personality. For her, it suitably accompanies his presence, just as Rachmaninoff provided the right mood for Laura's wistful memories of Alec. In the same vein, as Rosy begins to convince Charles, Lean alters the angle and, at intervals, enters totally into her frame of reference – as in the medium close shot of her with Charles' hand on her shoulder. At Rosy's eye level (face to face with her) and with Charles' head unseen, she now dominates the scene. A further effect of the pose – which recreates Alec's parting gesture in *Brief Encounter* – is the empathetic sense of urgency it instills in the audience, causing them,

216

despite whatever detached observations they may have previously made on Charles' 'Romantic' aspects, to side temporarily with Rosy and to ratify her quest of him as a husband.

Doryan's acutely disturbed state of mind demands to be conveyed by a more startling and extreme method. The split-second inserts of shells bursting open into black clouds of smoke and the whine of falling bombs over shot take the spectator inside Doryan's brain to participate in his affliction. Much as with Pip's collapse in *Great Expectations,* Lean gradually extends this visual and aural directness over the entire sequence of his fit of shaking in the pub: shuddering so intensely as he grips the bar that his drink tips over; an increasingly dense soundtrack full of discordant music and the noise of battle; the pounding, distorted sensory awareness translated into a wide-angle lens close shot of Michael's foot thumping against a bench. Finally, the withdrawal into a self-created world becomes so complete that when Doryan falls back mentally into the trenches, Lean records the inner event as if it were a real occurrence.

Part of what attracts Rosy to Doryan is his so obvious distress. A subsidiary consequence of synthesizing their meeting (of bringing down the lights on the set so that she literally reaches out to him in the dark) is to allow her adultery to become, in context, an act of charity as well as of personal gratification (and to retain, sympathetically, the audience's approval of her). But the other aspect, the sexual fulfilment, dominates Rosy's subsequent liaison with Doryan, usually through her eyes. The sexual interlude in the forest becomes a stylized externalization of her total experience, in body and thought. In her first glance of Doryan that day – a long shot of him on horseback – he is, like a knight errant before a castle or Childe Roland come to a dark tower, the graphic embodiment of all her past Romantic dreams. Similarly, the images intercut with the love-making in the arbor both emerge from and are selected by Rosy to form a montage of attraction not with the event *per se* but with her rapturous consciousness. The dandelion is Rose (the flower) ecstatically rent not by wind but by passion. The two silken strands of cobweb intertwining are Rosy's imagined out-of-the-body view of her form united with Doryan's. The shot of the sun (Doryan) hazily diffracted as the branches sway rhythmically overhead is multi-subjective: what Rosy sees as she lies on the ground below and what she feels at orgasm, the whole earth suddenly pulsing with her, swelling with her breath, heaving up with her cries, then slowly, tranquilly restoring itself.

Eventually, in Charles' personal vision of Rosy and Doryan on the beach, reality and illusion overlap completely: Charles projects their figures out of his imagination into the confines of his own concrete world (or, into the same two-dimensional frame he occupies). Unlike Doryan's flashback to the war zone, this manifestation is not part of any psychological disorder but arises purely from anxiety and suspicion. Neither is it a memory of something which has been witnessed or felt – it visualizes what, to Charles, can only be speculation. At this point, the audience has a fuller grasp of the situation than he does (knows that Rosy's affair is a fact, that it *was* probably she and Doryan walking on the sand) – their narrative awareness is not advanced here. But by implementing Charles' viewpoint, their knowledge of other factors is. Primarily, information is conveyed about Charles' character (as was, obviously, also the case with Rosy's experience in the forest, but then more was already known about her character than about Charles' at this moment). The degree of mental anguish felt is graphically implied in the clarity of the image he creates, while its style reveals his romanticizing nature (the iris of gauze he places over Rosy and Doryan's graceful motion across the open ground; the light breeze he expects would rustle her dress). Although he may magnify the incidentals slightly (the score, a stately mock-Beethoven, is his idea of 'romantic' music; the shell Doryan digs out for Rosy by the tide pool is later discovered in her drawer but is somewhat smaller than imagined), his general response – distressed but controlled, and not accusatory when he questions Rosy on her whereabouts – re-affirms his moral strength and, to some extent, his self-effacement, even under stress. Second, by relating two of Rosy's 'excursions' with Doryan in a subjective manner (first through Rosy, then through Charles), Lean totally justifies departing from objective

218

observation into an idealized, almost lyrical treatment of the affair, makes the point, in fact, in a way he could not before, that Rosy and Charles both tend to idealize and to 'dream' events.

Ryan's Daughter is perhaps the least ironic of Lean's motion pictures – not necessarily in the sense of plot (where Rosy's concealment of her father's guilt might qualify) but in terms of an enforced mood. There are some instances in the dialogue (the wry double-entendre in Rosy's explanation of why her skirt is soiled after riding with Doryan: 'Princess [meaning her horse] took a fall;' or Moureen's jibe at the masquerading Michael, 'Oh, Major darling, let me touch your V.C. You see my husband hasn't got one.'); but they make no thematic impression. Probably the most ironically revealing remark is in Father Hugh's parting words to Charles and Rosy, when he offers them a relic for a keepsake, 'It's supposed to be a fragment of St. Patrick's staff. I don't suppose it is, though.'

Generally, however, Lean limits ironic usage to certain devices in his editing. In the first scene between Charles and Rosy, for example, he injects dramatic apprehension fairly directly. Rosy's infatuation is as painfully obvious from her cosmetic preparations (even discarding her old shawl) and her attempt at striking a sophisticated air, as it is in her upset when Charles recounts that he met a 'stimulatin' woman' on his trip. Holding on a travelling two-shot as they walk, then tightening on Rosy as Charles describes how he and this woman attended a concert in Dublin ('She had the score'), and delaying the expected cut-away to Charles until he also mentions that 'she'd been at the teachin' for over fifty years,' heightens and releases tension in empathy with Rosy.

The first close look at Doryan is more complex. The cutting re-asserts the importance (already suggested by its position in the continuity) of his arrival, as staggered medium long, medium, medium close, and close shots draw the audience in on him, spatially *and* meditatively. They are manipulated into an anticipation of his face, made to scrutinize it as if there were something unusually noteworthy or striking in it. But Doryan just stares; his expression does not change or surprise; and after setting

219

the viewer up in this manner, the close shot of his boot does not elicit the pity it might have (because of subliminal resentment at being misled). Reflectively, the previous cuts prevent the audience from feeling pathos which might have undermined their acceptance of Doryan as larger-than-life and subsequently of Rosy's attraction to him (just as their rapid, dramatic succession does not allow the viewer time to adjust, to observe Doryan and gradually build-up an empathy which might subvert their identification with Rosy).

If any, the real irony is that while Lean may appear, on occasion, to be superficially detached from the action, his images – intercut and overlaid – constantly underscore the picture's directions and conflicts. One short sequence of two shots, such as that which occurs late in the film after Charles' disappearance, can summarize almost all of them: Father Hugh has just left Rosy after promising an apostolic search for Charles the following day. A close shot captures Rosy's uncertainty – she doesn't know yet if she wants Charles to return and yet (he is so basically a part of her) cannot think *beyond* his being there. Her face is side-lit: the left, dark as if favoring the colorations (and more sinister intimations) of Doryan; the right side is a soft gray as if gently radiant in Charles' presence. Still characterizing in this way Rosy's inner dilemma, her whole face is suddenly illuminated by a dissolve to the shore – the bright sand coalescing with her features, as if she were in free flight over it, searching anew for her destiny. Receding at the tide's edge are Charles' footprints, which she walked in once and which, it is inferred for an instant, she will choose to follow again. But after a moment, a shadow falls across them, Doryan's shadow – and nothing is resolved.

*　　*　　*　　*　　*

It is no easier at this point than it was at the beginning of this study to classify Lean's directorial style. As regards his handling of actors (which has been little spoken of before), the performances he guides in *Ryan's Daughter* are typical: carefully molded, pared of unnecessary outbursts, more given to understatement, to re-action shots and the impact of looks rather than words. Trevor Howard, the 'other man' of previous films, as Father Hugh – a part which could easily have verged on caricature – creating a truly human portrait; John Mills, a long way from Pip with make-up and mannerisms recalling Lon Chaney's Quasimodo, as Michael wandering poignantly about Kirrary; Christopher Jones as the spectral Major Doryan; Leo McKern as the guilt-ridden publican, Ryan; Robert Mitchum in an unusual role as the solid but unexciting school-teacher; and, finally, Sarah Miles as the child-like Rosy and the proud 'Princess,' ranging from innocent expectation to womanly passion – all are exceptionally drawn characters. It should be noted that Lean has displayed a penchant in his casting for using the faces of young, relative unknowns like Christopher Jones as often as those of old veterans like Mitchum. The list of current star performers to whom Lean gave the 'first break' is a long one, which includes names such as Peter O'Toole, Omar Sharif, Alec Guinness, and Trevor Howard. For Lean prides himself on selecting actors with regard to fitting the part rather than bolstering the box-office and has therefore never come to rely on a system of stars. If anything, Lean creates his own.

Technically, Lean constantly re-applies the early lessons of the cutting-room – his narrative remains direct, his exposition visual rather than verbal; his films still proceed without false starts and avoid needless interludes even in their three hour plus running times. Like Griffith, Ford, or Renoir, his composition might be termed 'classically' perfect. But his Pantheistic symbolism, his heroes – whether determined visionaries or emotional dreamers – and his figurative images mark Lean more as an inheritor of the Romantic tradition, which his thematic fixations from *Brief Encounter* to *Ryan's Daughter* confirm. If Lean has any stylistic trademark, beyond this tradition, it is in his concentration on the subjective aspects of film, in his exploitation of audience empathy and externalization of his characters' thought or feelings for dramatic effect.

Quite obviously, neither *Ryan's Daughter* nor any of Lean fourteen other motion pictures were fashioned as objects for critical assessment, but as personal works communicating equally personal conceptions

221

which demand acceptance or rejection on an individual basis. As we suggested earlier, the approximate insights of formal analysis (which may at best offer 'possible' interpretations) or, in this particular instance, the verses of Yeats (which may capture something analogous to the 'sensation' of *Ryan's Daughter*) can never really recreate a single frame. Perhaps the last thing to try to convey then, about this film and about David Lean, is the sense and appeal of the Romantic other world which they momentarily conjure up; and for that Yeats will serve best:

> Come away, oh human child
> To the waters and the wild . . .
> For the world's more full of weeping
> than you can understand.

Appendix

Bio-Filmography

Born March 25, 1908 at Croydon, England of Quaker parentage. Thrice married (to Kay Walsh, 1940-1949; Ann Todd, 1949-1957; and Leila Devi, 1960).

1927: Began work in the film industry as a tea boy at Gaumont. Worked as a clapper boy and messenger on Maurice Elvey's production of *Quinneys*. Worked variously in the following years as cutting room assistant, assistant cameraman, and assistant director.

1930: Chief-Editor of Gaumont-British News.

1931-1935: Editor of
- (1) British Movietonews (also occasionally writing and speaking commentary)
- (2) Paramount-British News
- (3) Various 'Quota-quickie' productions and re-issues with synchronized effects.

Major Films as Editor (and, at times, Assistant Director):

> *Escape Me Never* (Paul Czinner) 1935
>
> *As You Like It* (Paul Czinner) 1936
>
> *Pygmalion* (Anthony Asquith, Leslie Howard) 1938
>
> *French Without Tears* (Anthony Asquith) 1939
>
> *Major Barbara* (Gabriel Pascal, Harold French) 1941
>
> *49th Parallel* (Michael Powell) 1941
>
> *One Of Our Aircraft Is Missing* (Michael Powell,
> Emeric Pressburger) 1942

1942-1950:   With Ronald Neame and Anthony Havelock-Allan, part of the Cineguild 'triumvirate.' Work as director and in various phases of production on other Cineguild projects (generally uncredited).

1950-1962:   Work for Korda's London Films, Lopert, and Sam Spiegel's Horizon Pictures. Several unrealized projects including an adaptation of Paul Gallico's *The Snow Goose* and a biography of Galileo. Also *The Slave* (with Julie Christie) and *The Battle of Berlin* (1967).

1965:   Lean directed a number of scenes with Jose Ferrer and Claude Rains for *The Greatest Story Ever Told* as a favor to George Stevens.

In Which We Serve (1942)

Directors:	Noel Coward, David Lean
Producer:	Noel Coward
Associate Producer:	Anthony Havelock-Allan
Screenplay and Music:	Noel Coward
Photography:	Ronald Neame
Art Direction:	David Rawsley
Sound:	C. C. Stephens
Production Manager:	Sidney Streeter
Editors:	David Lean, Thelma Myers

Cast: Noel Coward (Captain Kinross), Bernard Miles (Chief Petty Officer Walter Hardy), John Mills (Ordinary Seaman Shorty Blake), Celia Johnson (Mrs. Kinross), Kay Walsh (Freda Lewis), Joyce Carey (Mrs. Hardy), Derek Elphinstone (Number One), Robert Sansom ('Guns'), Philip Friend ('Torps'), Michael Wilding ('Flags'), Hubert Gregg (Pilot), Ballard Berkeley (Engineer Commander), James Donald (Doctor), Kenneth Carton (Sub-Lieutenant R.N.V.R.), Walter Fitzgerald (Colonel Lumsden), Gerald Case (Captain Jasper Fry), Ann Stephens (Lavinia), Kathleen Harrison (Mrs. Blake), George Carney (Mr. Blake), Richard Attenborough (Young Sailor), Juliet Mills (Freda's baby).

Running time: 115 minutes

Distribution: British Lion (Great Britain); United Artists (United States)

Released: September, 1942 (G.B.); October, 1942 (U.S.)

*   *   *   *   *

This Happy Breed (1944)

Producer:	Noel Coward [Two Cities-Cineguild for Prestige-J. Arthur Rank]

In Charge of Production:	Anthony Havelock-Allan
Screenplay:	Noel Coward, from his play
Adaptation:	David Lean, Ronald Neame, Anthony Havelock-Allan
Photography:	Ronald Neame (*Technicolor*)
Camera Operator:	Guy Green
Color Directors:	Natalie Kalmus, Joan Bridge, Harold Hayson
Sound:	C. C. Stevens, John Cooke, Desmond Dew
Conductor:	Muir Matheson (London Symphony Orchestra)
Art Direction:	C. P. Norman
Art Supervisor to Coward:	G. E. Calthrop
Editor:	Jack Harris
Production Managers:	Ken Horne, Jack Martin
Assistant Director:	George Pollock
Dress Supervisor:	Hilda Collins
Make-up:	Tony Sforzini
Hair dressing:	Vivienne Walker
Special Effects:	Percy Day

Cast: Robert Newton (Frank Gibbons), Celia Johnson (Ethel Gibbons), John Mills (Billy Mitchell), Kay Walsh (Queenie Gibbons), Stanley Holloway (Bob Mitchell), Amy Veness (Mrs. Flint), Alison Leggatt (Aunt Sylvia), Eileen Erskine (Vi Gibbons), John Blythe (Reg Gibbons), Guy Verney (Sam Leadbitter), Merle Tottenham (Edie), Betty Fleetwood (Phyllis Blake).

Running Time: 107 minutes
Distribution: Eagle-Lion (G.B.); Universal-International (U.S.)
Released: June, 1944 (G.B.); April, 1947 (U.S.)

Blithe Spirit (1945)

Producer:	Noel Coward [Two Cities-Cineguild Rank]
Screenplay:	Noel Coward, from his play
Adaptation:	David Lean, Ronald Neame, Anthony Havelock-Allan
Photography:	Ronald Neame (*Technicolor*)
Special Effects:	Tom Howard
Color Directors:	Natalie Kalmus, Joan Bridge (Associate)
Sound:	John Cooke, Desmond Dew
Music:	Richard Addinsell
Conductor:	Muir Matheson (London Symphony Orchestra)
Art Direction:	C. P. Norman
Art Supervisor to Coward:	G. E. Calthrop
Editor:	Jack Harris
Unit Managers:	Norman Spencer, S. S. Streeter
Assistant Director:	George Pollock
Costumes:	Rahvia
Dress Supervisor:	Hilda Collins
Make-up:	Tony Sforzini
Hair dressing:	Vivienne Walker

Cast: Rex Harrison (Charles Condomine), Constance Cummings (Ruth), Kay Hammond (Elvira), Margaret Rutherford (Madame Arcati), Joyce Carey (Mrs. Bradman), Hugh Wakefield (Doctor Bradman), Jacqueline Clark (Edith).

Running time: 97 minutes
Distribution: General Film Distributors (G.B.); United Artists (U.S.)
Released: April, 1945 (G.B.); September, 1945 (U.S.)

Brief Encounter (1945)

Producer:	Noel Coward [Cineguild-Prestige-Rank]
Executives in charge of Production:	Anthony Havelock-Allan, Ronald Neame
Screenplay:	David Lean, Ronald Neame, Anthony Havelock-Allan, based on Noel Coward's play, *Still Life*
Adaptation:	Noel Coward
Photography:	Robert Krasker
Camera Operator:	B. Francke
Sound:	Stanley Lambourne, Desmond Dew
Music:	Rachmaninoff's 'Second Piano Concerto,' played by Eileen Joyce
Conductor:	Muir Matheson (National Symphony Orchestra)
Art Direction:	L. P. Williams
Art Supervisor to Coward:	G. E. Calthrop
Editor:	Jack Harris
Associate Editor:	Harry Miller
Production Manager:	E. Holding
Assistant Director:	George Pollock
Continuity:	Margaret Sibley

Cast: Celia Johnson (Laura Jesson), Trevor Howard (Dr. Alec Harvey), Cyril Raymond (Fred Jesson), Joyce Carey (Barmaid), Stanley Holloway (Station Guard), Valentine Dyall (Stephen Lynn), Everley Gregg (Dolly Messiter), Margaret Barton (Beryl), Dennis Harkin (Stanley).

Running time: 85 minutes

Distribution: Eagle-Lion (G.B.); Universal (U.S.)

Released: November, 1945 (G.B.); August, 1946 (U.S.)

Great Expectations (1946)

Producer:	Ronald Neame [Cineguild-Rank]
Executive Producer:	Anthony Havelock-Allan
Screenplay:	David Lean, Ronald Neame, Anthony Havelock-Allan with Kay Walsh and Cecil McGivern, based on the novel by Charles Dickens
Photography:	Guy Green
Camera Operator:	Nigel Huke
Sound:	Stanley Lambourne, Desmond Dew, Gordon K. McCallum
Music:	Walter Goehr, Kenneth Pakeman, G. Linley
Art Direction:	Wilfred Shingleton
Production Designer:	John Bryan
Conductor:	Walter Goehr (National Symphony Orchestra)
Editor:	Jack Harris
Production Manager:	Norman Spencer
Costumes:	Sophie Harris [Motley], Margaret Furse (Assistant)
Continuity:	Margaret Sibley
Choreography:	Suria Magito

Cast: John Mills ('Pip'), Valerie Hobson (Estella), Bernard Miles (Joe Gargery), Francis L. Sullivan (Jaggers), Finlay Currie (Magwitch), Martita Hunt (Miss Havisham), Anthony Wager ('Pip' as a boy), Jean Simmons (Estella as a girl), Alec Guinness (Herbert Pocket), Ivor Barnard (Wemmick), Freda Jackson (Mrs. Joe Gargery), Torin Thatcher (Bentley Drummle), Eileen Erskine (Biddy), Hay Petrie

(Uncle Pumblychook), George Hayes (Compeyson), Richard George (the Sergeant), Everley Gregg (Sarah Pocket), John Burch (Mr. Wopsle), Grace Denbigh-Russell (Mrs. Wopsle), O. B. Clarence (the Aged Parent), John Forrest (the Pale Young Gentleman), Anne Holland (a Relation), Frank Atkinson (Mike), Gordon Begg (Night Porter), Edie Martin (Mrs. Whimple), Walford Hyden (the Dancing Master), Roy Arthur (Galley Steersman).

Running time: 115 minutes
Distribution: General Film Distributors (G.B.); Universal-International (U.S.)
Released: December, 1946 (G.B.); May, 1947 (U.S.)

* * * * *

Oliver Twist (1948)

Producer:	Ronald Neame [Cineguild-J. Arthur Rank]
Screenplay:	David Lean, Stanley Haynes, from the novel by Charles Dickens
Photography:	Guy Green
Camera Operator:	Oswald Morris
Sound:	Stanley Lambourne, G. K. McCallum
Music:	Sir Arnold Bax
Conductor:	Muir Matheson (Philharmonic Orchestra of London); solo pianoforte, Harriet Cohen
Art Direction:	John Bryan
Editor:	Jack Harris
Production Manager:	Norman Spencer
Assistant Director:	George Pollock

Costumes: Margaret Furse
Make-up: Stuart Freebourne
Continuity: Margaret Sibley

Cast: Robert Newton (Bill Sikes), Alec Guinness (Fagin), Kay Walsh
    (Nancy), John Howard Davies (Oliver), Francis L. Sullivan (Mr.
    Bumble), Henry Stephenson (Mr. Brownlow), Mary Clare (the
    Matron), Anthony Newley (the Artful Dodger), Josephine Stuart
    (Oliver's mother), Ralph Truman (Monks), Gibb McLaughlin (Mr.
    Sowerberry), Amy Veness (Mrs. Bedwin), Frederick Lloyd (Mr.
    Grimwig), Henry Edwards (Police Official), Ivor Barnard (Chair-
    man of the Board), Maurice Denham (Chief of Police), Michael Dear
    (Noah Claypole), Michael Ripper (Barney), Peter Bull (Landlord of
    the 'Three Cripples'), Deirdre Doyle (Mrs. Thingummy), Diana
    Dors (Charlotte), Kenneth Downy (Workhouse Master), W. G. Fay
    (Bookseller), Edie Martin (Annie), Gravely Edwards (Mr. Fang),
    John Potter (Charley Bates), Maurice Jones (Workhouse Doctor),
    Hattie Jacques, Betty Paul (Sings at the 'Three Cripples').

Running time: 116 minutes (G.B.); 104 minutes (U.S.)
Distribution: Eagle-Lion (G.B.); United Artists (U.S.)
Released: June, 1948 (G.B.); July, 1951 (U.S.)

*   *   *   *   *

The Passionate Friends
[One Woman's Story (U.S.)] *(1949)*

Producer: Ronald   Neame   [Cineguild-J.
                                    Arthur Rank]
Screenplay: Eric Ambler, based on the novel
                                    by H. G. Wells

Adaptation:	David Lean, Stanley Haynes
Photography:	Oswald Morris
Sound:	F. G. Hugheson
Production Designer:	John Bryan
Set Decorator:	Claude Manusey
Editors:	Jack Harris (Supervising), Geoffrey Foot
Assistant Director:	George Pollock
Costumes:	Margaret Furse

Cast: Ann Todd (Mary Justin), Trevor Howard (Steven Stratton), Claude
Rains (Howard Justin), Isabel Dean (Pat), Betty Ann Davies (Miss
Layton), Arthur Howard (man-servant), Guido Lorraine (Hotel
Manager), Marcel Poncin (Hall Porter), Natasha Sokolova (Cham-
bermaid), Helen Buris (Flowerwoman), Jean Serrett (Emigration
Official), Frances Waring (Charwoman), Wanda Rogerson (2nd
Bridge Guest), Wilfred Hyde-White (Solicitor).

Running time: 87 minutes

Distribution: General Film Distributors (G.B.); Universal-International
(U.S.)

Released: January, 1949 (G.B.); June, 1949 (U.S.)

*   *   *   *   *

Madeleine (1950)

Producer:	Stanley Haynes [and David Lean for Cineguild-J. Arthur Rank]
Screenplay:	Nicholas Phipps, Stanley Haynes, based on the actual case of Madeleine Hamilton Smith
Photography:	Guy Green
Music:	William Alwyn

Conductor: Muir Matheson (Royal Philar-
                                              monic Orchestra)
Editor: Geoffrey Foot
Costumes: Margaret Furse
Assistant Director: George Pollock
Art Direction: John Bryan

Cast: Ann Todd (Madeleine Smith), Ivan Desny (Emile L'Angelier),
    Norman Woland (William Minnoch), Leslie Banks (Mr. Smith),
    Barbara Everest (Mrs. Smith), Susan Stranks (Janet Smith), Patricia
    Raine (Bessie Smith), Elizabeth Sellars (Christina), Edward Chap-
    man (Doctor Thompson), Jean Cadell (Mrs Jenkins), Eugene
    Deckers (Monsieur Thuau), Ivor Barnard (Mr. Murdoch), David
    Horne (Lord Justice), Harry Jones (Lord Advocate), Andre Morell
    (Dean of Faculty), Henry Edwards (Clerk of the Court), Amy
    Veness (Miss Aiken), John Laurie (Scots Divine), Kynaston Reeves
    (Dr. Penny), Cameron Hall (Dr. Yeoman), Douglas Barr (William),
    Irene Brown (Mrs. Grant), Alfred Rodriguez, Moira Fraser
    (Highland Dancers), James McKechnie (Narrator).

Running time: 114 minutes
Distribution: General Film Distributors (G.B.); Walter Reade and
                 Universal-International (U.S.).
Released: February, 1950 (G.B.); September, 1950 (U.S.)

                    *   *   *   *   *

The Sound Barrier [alternate titles:
Breaking Through The Sound Barrier (G.B.);
Breaking The Sound Barrier (U.S.)] (1952)

Producer: David Lean [London Films]
Screenplay: Terence Rattigan

Photography:	Jack Hildyard; John Wilcox, Peter Newbrook, Jo Jago (Aerial Sequences)
Music:	Malcolm Arnold
Conductor:	Muir Matheson (London Philharmonic Orchestra)
Art Direction:	Vincent Korda; Joseph Bato, John Hawkesworth
Production Manager:	John Palmer
Associate Producer:	Norman Spencer
Editor:	Geoffrey Foot
Aerial Unit Director:	Anthony Squire

Cast: Ralph Richardson (Sir John Ridgefield), Ann Todd (Susan Ridgefield Garthwaite), Nigel Patrick (Tony Garthwaite), John Justin (Philip Peel), Dinah Sheridan (Jess Peel), Joseph Tomelty (Will Sparks), Denholm Elliott (Chris Ridgefield), Jack Allen (Windy Williams), Ralph Michael (Fletcher), Douglas Muir, Leslie Philips (Controllers), Robert Brooks Turner (Test Bed Operator), Anthony Snell (Peter Makepeace), Jolyon Jackley (John), Vincent Holman (A.T.A. Officer); And the de Havilland *Comet* and *Vampire;* the Vickers-Supermarine *Attacker.*

Running time: 118 minutes
Distribution: British Lion (G.B.); Lopert Films/United Artists (U.S.)
Released: July, 1952 (G.B.); November, 1952 (U.S.)

*   *   *   *   *

Hobson's Choice (1954)

Producer:	David Lean [London Films]
Associate Producer:	Norman Spencer

Screenplay:	David Lean, Norman Spencer, Wynard Browne, based on the play by Harold Brighouse
Photography:	Jack Hildyard
Camera Operator:	Peter Newbrook
Sound:	John Cox (Supervising), Buster Ambler, Red Law
Music:	Malcolm Arnold
Conductor:	Muir Matheson (Royal Philharmonic Orchestra)
Editor:	Peter Taylor
Production Manager:	John Palmer
Assistant Director:	Adrian Pryce-Jones
Costumes:	John Armstrong, Julia Squire
Make-up:	Tony Sforzini, George Parleton
Hair dressing:	Gladys Atkinson
Continuity:	Margaret Shipway

Cast: Charles Laughton (Henry Hobson), Brenda de Banzie (Maggie), John Mills (Willie Mossop), Daphne Anderson (Alice Hobson), Prunella Scales (Vicky Hobson), Richard Wattis (Albert Prosser), Derek Blomfield (Freddy Beenstock), Helen Haye (Mrs. Hepworth), Joseph Tomelty (Jim Heeler), Julien Mitchell (Sam Minns), Gibb McLaughlin (Tudsbury), Philip Stainton (Denton), Dorothy Gordon (Ada Figgins), Madge Brindley (Mrs. Figgins), John Laurie (Dr. McFarlane), Raymond Huntley (Mr. Beenstock), Jack Howarth (Tubby Wadlow), Herbert C. Walton (Printer).

Running time: 107 minutes
Distribution: British Lion (G.B.); United Artists (U.S.)
Released: March, 1954 (G.B.); June, 1954 (U.S.)

Summer Madness
[Summertime (U.S.)] (1955)

Producer:	Ilya Lopert
Assistant Producer:	Norman Spencer
Screenplay:	David Lean, H. E. Bates, based on the play, *Time of the Cuckoo,* by Arthur Laurents
Photography:	Jack Hildyard *(Technicolor)*
Camera Operator:	Peter Newbrook
Sound:	Peter Handford, John Cox
Music:	Alessandro Cicognini; Rossini's "La Gazza Ladra" (Recorded in Rome)
Art Direction:	Vincent Korda; Bill Hutchinson, Ferdinand Bellan (Assistants)
Editor:	Peter Taylor
Production Managers:	Raymond Anzarut, Franco Magli
Production Assistant:	Robert J. Kingsley
Assistant Directors:	Adrian Pryce-Jones, Alberto Cardone
Make-up:	Cesare Gamberelli
Hair dressing:	Gracia de Rossi
Continuity:	Margaret Shipway

Cast: Katharine Hepburn (Jane Hudson), Rossano Brazzi (Renato Di Rossi), Isa Miranda (Signora Fiorina), Darren McGavin (Eddie Jaeger), Mari Aldon (Phyl Jaeger), Jane Rose (Edith McIlhenny), MacDonald Parke (Lloyd McIlhenny), Gaetano Audiero (Mauro), Andre Morell (Englishman on train), Jeremy Spencer (Vito), Virginia Simeon (Giovanna).

Running time: 99 minutes
Distribution: Lopert Films/United Artists
Released: May, 1955 (G.B.); June, 1955 (U.S.)
Filmed on location in Venice

*   *   *   *   *

The Bridge On The River Kwai (1957)

Producer:	Sam Spiegel [Horizon Pictures-Columbia]
Screenplay:	Pierre Boulle; Michael Wilson, Carl Foreman (uncredited), based on Boulle's novel
Photography:	Jack Hildyard *(Technicolor; Cinemascope)*
Camera Operator:	Peter Newbrook
Sound:	John Cox, John Mitchell
Music:	Malcolm Arnold; 'Colonel Bogey March' by Kenneth J. Alford (Royal Philharmonic Orchestra)
Art Direction:	Donald M. Ashton; Geoffrey Drake (Assistant)
Editor:	Peter Taylor
Production Manager:	Cecil F. Ford
Production Executive:	William N. Graf
Assistant Directors:	Gus Agosti, Ted Sturgis
Construction Manager:	Peter Dukelow
Technical Advisor:	Major-General L. E. M. Perowne
Consulting Engineers:	Husband and Company, Sheffield. Bridge constructed by Equipment and Construction Company, Ceylon.

Wardrobe:	John Apperson
Continuity:	Angela Martelli

Cast: Alec Guinness (Colonel Nicholson), William Holden (Shears), Jack Hawkins (Major Warden), Sessue Hayakawa (Colonel Saito), James Donald (Dr. Clipton), Geoffrey Horne (Lieutenant Joyce), Andre Morell (Colonel Green), Peter Williams (Captain Reeves), John Boxer (Major Hughes), Percy Herbert (Grogan), Harold Goodwin (Baker), Ann Sears (Nurse), Henry Okawa (Captain Kanematsu), K. Katsumoto (Lieutenant Miura), M. R. B. Chakrabanhu (Yai), Viliaiwan Seeboonreaung, Ngamta Suphaphongs, Javanart Punychoti, Kannikar Dowklee (Siamese Girls).

Running time: 161 minutes

Distribution: Columbia Pictures

Released: November, 1957

Filmed on location in Ceylon. Approximately one year in production with a budget of 3,000,000 dollars.

*　　*　　*　　*　　*

Lawrence of Arabia (1962)

Producer:	Sam Spiegel [Horizon Pictures-Columbia]
Screenplay:	Robert Bolt, Michael Wilson (uncredited), based on various writings by and about T. E. Lawrence
Photography:	Fred A. Young (*Technicolor; Super Panavision 70*)
Camera Operator:	Ernest Day
Second Unit Cameramen:	Skeets Kelly, Nicolas Roeg, Peter Newbrook

Sound:	Paddy Cunningham
Music:	Maurice Jarre; 'The Voice of the Guns' by Kenneth J. Alford; arrangements by Gerard Shurman
Musical Co-ordinator:	Morris Stoloff
Conductor:	Sir Adrian Boult (London Philharmonic Orchestra)
Production Designer:	John Box
Art Direction:	John Stoll
Assistant Art Directors:	Roy Rossotti, George Richardson, Terry Marsh, Anthony Rimmington
Set Decoration:	Dario Simoni
Editor:	Anne Coates
Production Manager:	John Palmer
Assistant Director:	Roy Stevens
Second Unit Directors:	Andre Smagghe, Noel Howard
Casting Director:	Maude Spector
Construction Managers:	Peter Dukelow; Fred Bennett (Asst.)
Location Manager:	Douglas Twiddy
Property Master:	Eddie Fowlie
Costumes:	Phyllis Dalton
Wardrobe:	John Apperson
Make-up:	Charles Parker
Hair dressing:	A. G. Scott
Continuity:	Barbara Cole

Cast: Peter O'Toole (Thomas Edward Lawrence), Alec Guinness (Prince Feisal), Anthony Quinn (Auda), Jack Hawkins (General Allenby), Omar Sharif (Sherif Ali), Anthony Quayle (Colonel Brighton), Claude Rains (Mr. Dryden), Arthur Kennedy (Jackson Bentley), Jose Ferrer (Turkish Bey), Donald Wolfit (General Murray), I. S. Johar (Gasim), Gamil Ratib (Majid), Michael Ray (Farraj), Zia

241

Mohyeddin (Tafas), John Dimech (Daud), Howard Marion Craw-ford (Medical Officer), Jack Gwillim (Club Secretary), Hugh Miller (R.A.M.C. Colonel).

Running time: 221 minutes (in Roadshow engagements); 200 minutes in General Release [cut by Spiegel. 184 minutes in 1971 U.S. re-issue]

Distribution: Columbia Pictures

Released: December, 1962

Filmed on location in Jordan, Spain, Morocco, and England. Approximately three years in production with a budget of 15,000,000 dollars.

*   *   *   *   *

Doctor Zhivago (1965)

Producer:	Carlo Ponti (Metro-Goldwyn-Mayer)
Executive Producer:	Arvid L. Griffen
Screenplay:	Robert Bolt, based on the novel by Boris Pasternak
Photography:	Fred A. Young *(Metrocolor; Panavision)*
Camera Operator:	Ernest Day
Second Unit Cameraman:	Manuel Berenguer
Sound:	Paddy Cunningham
Re-recording:	Franklin Milton, William Steinkamp
Music:	Maurice Jarre (conducted by the composer)
Production Designer·	John Box
Art Direction:	Terence Marsh; Gil Parrondo (Associate)

Assistant Art Directors:	Ernest Archer, Bill Hutchinson, Roy Walker
Set Decoration:	Dario Simoni
Editor:	Norman Savage
Production Supervisor:	John Palmer
Production Managers:	Augustin Pastor, Douglas Twiddy
Assistant Directors:	Roy Stevens, Pedro Vidal
Second Unit Director:	Roy Rossotti
Dialogue Coach:	Hugh Miller
Costumes:	Phyllis Dalton
Make-up:	Mario van Riel
Hair dressing:	Gracia de Rossi, Anna Christofani
Continuity:	Barbara Cole
Special Effects:	Eddie Fowlie
M.G.M. Representative:	Stanley H. Goldsmith

Cast: Omar Sharif (Yuri Zhivago), Julie Christie (Lara), Geraldine Chaplin (Tonya Gromeko Zhivago), Tom Courtenay (Pasha/Strelnikov), Alec Guinness (General Yegraf Zhivago), Siobhan McKenna (Anna Gromeko), Ralph Richardson (Alexander Gromeko), Rod Steiger (Komarovsky), Rita Tushingham (The Girl, Tonya), Adrienne Corri (Lara's Mother), Geoffrey Keen (Professor Kurt), Jeffrey Rockland (Sasha Zhivago), Lucy Westmore (Katya), Noel William (Razin), Gerard Tichy (Liberius), Klaus Kinski (Kostoyed), Jack MacGowran (Petya), Maria Martin (Gentlewoman), Tarek Sharif (Yuri at age Eight), Mercedes Ruiz (Tonya at age Seven), Roger Maxwell (Colonel in charge of Replacements), Inigo Jackson (Major), Virgilio Texeira (Captain), Bernard Kay (Bolshevik Deserter), Erik Chitty (Old Soldier), Jose Nieto (the Priest), Mark Eden (Young Engineer), Emilio Carrer (Mr. Sventytski), Gerhard Jersch (David), Wolf Frees (Comrade Yelkin), Gwen Nelson (Comrade Kaprugina), Jose Caffarel (Militiaman), Brigitte Trace (Streetwalker), Luana Alcaniz (Mrs. Sventytski), Lili

Murati, Catherine Ellison, Maria Vico (Women), D. Assad Bahador (Dragoon Colonel), Peter Madden (Political Officer).

Running time: 197 minutes [at New York premiere]; 180 minutes after studio cut.

Distribution: Metro-Goldwyn-Mayer

Released: December, 1965 (U.S.); April, 1966 (G.B.)

Filmed on location in Spain, Finland, and Canada. Approximately three years in production with a budget of 12,000,000 dollars.

*   *   *   *   *

Ryan's Daughter (1970)

Producer:	Anthony Havelock-Allan [Faraway Productions AG Film-M.G.M.]
Associate Producer:	Roy Stevens
Screenplay:	Robert Bolt
Photography:	Fred A. Young (*Metrocolor; Super Panavision*)
Camera Operator:	Ernest Day
Second Unit Cameramen:	Denys Coop, Robert Huke
Sound:	John Bramall
Re-recording:	Gordon K. McCallum; Eric Tomlinson (Music)
Music:	Maurice Jarre (conducted by the composer)
Production Designer	Stephen Grimes
Art Direction:	Roy Walker; Derek Irvine (assistant)
Set Decoration:	Josie MacAvin
Editor:	Norman Savage

Production Manager:	Douglas Twiddy
Assistant Directors:	Pedro Vidal, Michael Stevenson
Second Unit Directors:	Charles Frend, Roy Stevens (storm sequence)
Production Liaison:	William O'Kelly
Construction Manager:	Peter Dukelow
Location and Property Manager:	Eddie Fowlie
Costumes:	Jocelyn Rickards
Make-up:	Charles Parker
Hair dressing:	A. G. Scott
Continuity:	Phyllis Crocker
Special Effects:	Robert Macdonald

Cast: Sarah Miles (Rosy Ryan), Robert Mitchum (Charles Shaughnessy), Trevor Howard (Father Hugh Collins), Christopher Jones (Major Andrew Doryan), John Mills (Michael), Leo McKern (Tom Ryan), Barry Foster (Tim O'Leary), Marie Kean (Mrs. McCardle), Arthur O'Sullivan (Mr. McCardle), Evin Crowley (Moureen), Douglas Sheldon (Driver), Gerald Sim (Captain), Barry Jackson (Corporal), Des Keogh (Private), Niall Toibin (O'Keefe), Philip O'Flynn (Paddy), Donal Neligan (Moureen's Boyfriend), Brian O'Higgins (Constable O'Connor), Niall O'Brien (Bernard), Owen Sullivan (Joseph).

Running time: 196 minutes (Roadshow); 165 minutes (U.S. General release)

Distribution: Metro-Goldwyn-Mayer

Released: December, 1970

Filmed on location on the West Coast of Ireland and in North Africa. Approximately three years in production with a budget of 14,000,000 dollars.

Select Bibliography

Periodicals

Alpert, Hollis. 'The David Lean Recipe: A "Whack in the Guts".' NEW YORK TIMES MAGAZINE, May 23, 1965.

Alpert, Hollis. 'David Lean's Big Gamble.' SATURDAY REVIEW, November 14, 1970.

Blume, Mary. 'Lean directs his Films by fussing for Perfection.' LOS ANGELES TIMES, October 25, 1970.

Blume, Mary. 'A Brief Encounter with David Lean.' AFTER DARK, December, 1970.

FILMMAKER'S NEWSLETTER. 'An Interview with Robert Bolt.' Volume VI, number 12 (1973).

FILMS AND FILMING. 'Out of the Wilderness.' January, 1963.

Foreman, Carl. 'Confessions of a Frustrated Screenwriter.' FILM COMMENT, Volume 6, number 4.

Hill, Stephen P. 'Evaluating the Directors.' FILMS IN REVIEW, Volume 12, pp. 7-13.

Huntley, John. 'The Music of *Hamlet* and *Oliver Twist*.' PENGUIN FILM REVIEW, Number 8.

Lean, David. 'Brief Encounter.' PENGUIN FILM REVIEW, Number 4.

Lejeune, C. A. 'The Up and Coming Team . . .' NEW YORK TIMES, June 15, 1947.

LOS ANGELES HERALD EXAMINER. 'Flying Director.' February 7, 1971.

LOS ANGELES TIMES. 'British Cinema – Where is the life that once it led?' January 27, 1963.

McVay, Douglas. 'David Lean, Lover of Life.' FILMS AND FILMING, August, 1959.

Moss, Morton. 'How To Make a Movie.' LOS ANGELES HERALD EXAMINER, March 9, 1971

MOVIES INTERNATIONAL. 'David Lean, the Bitterest Loser of Them All.' Volume 1, number 3 [1966].

POPULAR PHOTOGRAPHY. 'What Can You Learn from Movies.' March, 1958. [Interview with Lean].

Price, Stanley. 'On the Spanish Steppes with Dr. Zhivago.' SHOW, May, 1965.

Ross, Stephen. 'David Lean.' TAKE ONE, Volume III, number 12, p. 10f.

SENIOR SCHOLASTIC. 'Movie Audiences Don't Change.' February 15, 1971. [Interview with Lean]

VARIETY (d). 'As Long as David Lean . . .' November 27, 1970.

Westerbeck, Colin L. 'The Lean Years.' COMMONWEAL, December 18, 1970.

Wolf, William. 'Lean Rejects Drawing Room Comedies.' LOS ANGELES TIMES, October 26, 1969.

Books

Charensol, Georges. LE CINEMA. Paris: Libraire Larousse (1966)

Cowie, Peter. A CONCISE HISTORY OF THE CINEMA. New Jersey: A. S. Barnes (1971)

Durgnat, Raymond. A MIRROR FOR ENGLAND: BRITISH MOVIES FROM AUSTERITY TO AFFLUENCE. New York – Washington: Praeger Publishers (1971).

Ford, Charles and Jeanne, Rene. HISTOIRE ENCYCLOPEDIQUE DU CINEMA. Paris: S.E.D.E. (1962)

Fulton, A. R. MOTION PICTURES. University of Oklahoma Press (1960)

Gubern, Roman. HISTORIA DEL CINE. Madrid: Ediciones Danae (1969)

Huntley, John. BRITISH TECHNICOLOR FILMS. London: Skelton – Robinson (1950)

Houston, Penelope. THE CONTEMPORARY CINEMA. Middlesex: Penguin (1964)

Jarvie, Ian C. MOVIES AND SOCIETY. New York: Basic Books (1970)

McClelland, Douglas. THE UNKINDEST CUTS. New Jersey: A. S. Barnes (1972)

Macgowan, Kenneth. BEHIND THE SCREEN. New York: Delacorte (1964)

Manvell, Roger. NEW CINEMA IN BRITAIN. London: Studio Vista/Dutton (1969).

Manvell, Roger. THE FILM AND THE PUBLIC. Middlesex: Penguin (1955).

Manvell, Roger. WHAT IS A FILM. London: Macdonald (1965).

Oakley, C. A. WHERE WE CAME IN – SEVENTY YEARS OF THE BRITISH FILM INDUSTRY. London: George, Allen, and Unwin.

Robinson, David. WORLD CINEMA: A SHORT HISTORY. London: Eyre Methuen (1973)

Rotha, Paul and Griffith, Richard. THE FILM TILL NOW. London: Vision Press (1949).

Sadoul, Georges. HISTOIRE DU CINEMA MONDIAL. Paris: Flammarion (1949).

Schickel, Richard. MOVIES. New York: Basic Books (1964)

Also: a documentary film, *David Lean: A Self-Portrait,* produced and directed by Thomas Craven.

An interview by Gerard Pratley for the Canadian Broadcasting Company is reproduced in Andrew Sarris, INTERVIEWS WITH FILM DIRECTORS (1967; Bobbs-Merrill).

Acknowledgements

Thanks, first of all, to David Bradley without whose kind assistance many of the chapters could not have been written.

Thanks also to Ron Garrison for aiding in the bibliographic research; Albert Hutter (and members of the class of English 164) for information on Dickens and ideas about the adaptations; to Don Adams for facilitating the frame enlargements; Elaine Hofstetter and Elmer Silver for helping prepare the final manuscript; and Nick Peterson, Evelyn Renold, Stan Berkowitz, Howard Suber, Phil Chamberlin, and Jim Paris.

Stills courtesy of United Artists, Universal, Metro-Goldwyn-Mayer, Columbia, and David Chierichetti.

Dedicated to a 'Rosy Ryan,' of our own.

A. S. & J. U.

Index

253